ENCOUN

MW01056434

15 Stirring Tales and Exciting Encounters

With Reading, Comprehension, Literature, and Writing SKILLS

by Burton Goodman

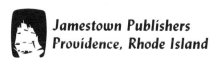

Jamestown Publishers
Providence, Rhode Island

Encounters

Catalog No. 777
© 1995 by Burton Goodman

Cover and text design by Patricia Volpe, adapted from the original
    design by Deborah Hulsey Christie
Cover illustration by Bob Eggleton

Text illustrations by
    Jan Naimo Jones: pp. 19, 59, 132; Pamela R. Levy: pp. 36, 94;
    David Opie: pp. 122–123; Lance Paladino: pp. 28–29, 70–71;
    Marcy Ramsey: pp. 45, 102–103; Joel Snyder: pp. 51, 78–79, 112;
    Adam Young: pp. 8–9, 87

Printed in the United States of America

1 2 3 4 5 BP 99 98 97 96 95

ISBN 0-89061-768-6

Contents

To the Student

$\mathcal{T}$his book contains 15 outstanding stories, each of recognized literary value. Within these pages you will find time-honored authors, as well as present-day writers. You will find, too, that many countries and cultures are represented.

As the title suggests, each selection in this volume involves an encounter. There are, of course, many different kinds of encounters. As you might expect, there are encounters with enemies and danger. But characters also look within themselves, as they encounter questions dealing with personal courage and conscience. All of these, and more, are presented here.

These stories will provide you with many hours of reading pleasure, and the exercises that follow offer a wide variety of ways to help you improve your reading and literature skills. In fact, the exercises have been specially designed with *skill* mastery in mind:

> SELECTING DETAILS FROM THE STORY
>
> KNOWING NEW VOCABULARY WORDS
>
> IDENTIFYING STORY ELEMENTS
>
> LOOKING AT CLOZE
>
> LEARNING HOW TO READ CRITICALLY

SELECTING DETAILS FROM THE STORY will help you improve your reading comprehension skills.

KNOWING NEW VOCABULARY WORDS will help you strengthen your vocabulary skills. Often, you will be able to figure out the meaning of an unfamiliar word by using *context clues*—the words and phrases around the word.

IDENTIFYING STORY ELEMENTS will give you practice in recognizing and understanding the key elements of literature.

LOOKING AT CLOZE will help you reinforce your reading *and* your vocabulary skills through the use of the cloze technique.

LEARNING HOW TO READ CRITICALLY will help you sharpen your critical thinking skills. You will have opportunities to *reason* by drawing conclusions, making inferences, using story clues, and so forth.

There are four questions in each of these exercises. Do all the exercises. Then check your answers with your teacher. Use the scoring chart following each exercise to calculate your score for that exercise. Give yourself 5 points for each correct answer.

Since there are four questions, you can receive up to 20 points for each exercise. Use the SKILL scoring chart at the end of the exercises to figure your total score. A perfect score for the exercises would equal 100 points. Keep track of how well you do by recording your score on the Progress Chart on page 140. Then record your score on the Progress Graph on page 141 to plot your progress.

Another section, **Improving Writing and Discussion Skills**, offers further opportunities for thoughtful discussion and creative writing.

On the following page, you will find brief definitions of some important literary terms. If you wish, refer to these definitions when you answer the questions in the section Identifying Story Elements.

I feel certain that you will enjoy reading the stories in this book. And the exercises that follow will help you master a number of very important skills.

Now . . . get ready for some *Encounters!*

Burton Goodman

The Short Story—Literary Terms

Character Development: the change in a character from the beginning to the conclusion of the story.

Characterization: the ways a writer shows what a character is like. The way a character acts, speaks, thinks, and looks *characterizes* that person.

Climax: the turning point of a story.

Conflict: a struggle or difference of opinion between characters. Sometimes a character may clash with a force of nature.

Dialogue: the exact words that a character says; usually the conversation between characters.

Foreshadowing: clues that hint or suggest what will happen later in the story.

Inner Conflict: a struggle that takes place in the mind of a character.

Main Character: the person the story is mostly about.

Mood: the feeling or atmosphere that the writer creates. For example, the *mood* of a story might be humorous or suspenseful.

Motive: the reason behind a character's actions.

Narrator: the person who tells the story. Usually, the *narrator* is the writer or a character in the story.

Plot: the series of incidents or happenings in a story. The *plot* is the outline or arrangement of events.

Purpose: the reason the author wrote the story. For example, an author's *purpose* might be to amuse or entertain, to convince, or to inform.

Setting: the time and place of the action in a story; where and when the action takes place.

Style: the way in which a writer uses language. The choice and arrangement of words and sentences help to create the writer's *style.*

Theme: the main, or central idea, of a story.

I. Three Skeleton Key

by George G. Toudouze

Meet the Author

George G. Toudouze (1877–1972) was born in Paris, France. His father, Gustave Toudouze, was a well-known writer of the time. As "Three Skeleton Key" suggests, Toudouze was fascinated with the sea. He wrote a history of the French navy, as well as numerous adventure novels. In addition to his many short stories, Toudouze wrote several plays and dozens of articles on travel and art.

*W*hat was my most terrifying experience? Well, one does have a few after thirty-five years of working at lighthouses. But let me answer your question.

When I was a young man just starting out, there was an opening on a lighthouse that had just been built off the coast of Guiana. This lighthouse stood on a jagged strip of rock twenty miles away from the mainland. The pay was high, and since I was determined to save a goodly sum before I got married, I volunteered for service there.

The rock on which the lighthouse stood was known as Three Skeleton Key. The place earned its name and its bad reputation from the story of three convicts who escaped from a jail in a stolen canoe. The canoe was wrecked on the rock during the night, and though the convicts managed to escape from the raging sea, they eventually died of hunger and thirst. When they were finally discovered on the rock, nothing remained but three heaps of bones picked clean by the birds. According to the tale, three skeletons, gleaming with light, danced over the rock, screaming.

But there are many such stories, and when I was told by old-timers about Three Skeleton Key, I ignored their warning. I signed up for the job, boarded a ship, and one month later I was installed at the lighthouse.

Picture the lighthouse—a tall gray cylinder welded to the solid rock by iron rods. Picture it rising into the air, twenty miles from land. Yes, this rock was actually an *island* in the midst of the sea, an island of rock, one hundred and fifty feet long and forty feet wide, just big enough to let you stretch your legs. But you had to be very careful when you walked about, for the stones on this island were extremely slippery. One misstep and you could fall into the sea. Not that the risk of drowning was so great—but the waters around the island swarmed with sharks.

Still, it was a nice life there. We had enough provisions to last until the supply ship came. During the day we worked in the lighthouse, polishing the metalwork and the lens and reflector of the great light itself. And at night we sat on the gallery and watched the light. We would stare at the powerful white beam as it swung over the sea from the top of our tower, one hundred and twenty feet high.

Others perhaps might have tired of that kind of life—stranded on a small island off the coast of South Africa for eighteen months at a time until your turn for shore leave came. But we found it pleasant enough, my two fellow lighthouse keepers and myself, so much so that after two years I was still greatly satisfied with the life on Three Skeleton Key.

I had just returned from shore leave at the end of June, and had settled into the routine with my two fellow keepers of the light, Le Gleo and Itchoua. Le Gleo was a Frenchman about my age, while Itchoua, the head keeper of the light, was from Spain and about ten years older than Le Gleo or I. It was Itchoua, on evening watch, who called us up to the gallery and pointed silently out to the sea.

In the distance we saw a huge three-master ship, with all its sails set, heading on a course straight for the lighthouse. That was very strange, for the vessel must surely have seen us! Each time our light passed, it lit up the ship with the glare of day.

Now ships were a rare sight indeed in our waters, for our light was a warning of treacherous reefs hidden under the surface. As a result, vessels always stayed a good distance away, especially large ships that cannot maneuver as readily as steamers.

No wonder then that we were shocked at seeing this three-master heading straight for us in the evening gloom. I could see that it was a beautiful ship, perhaps four thousand tons or so, a fast sailer that had carried cargo to every part of the world.

Le Gleo suddenly cried out, "What's wrong with its crew? Are they blind or insane? Can't they *see* us?"

Itchoua slowly nodded, then softly remarked, "See us? No doubt they can—if there *is* a crew on board."

"What do you mean, chief?" said Le Gleo. "Do you mean it's abandoned?"

Then we understood the vessel's strange behavior. Itchoua was right. For some reason, the crew, believing it doomed, had abandoned the vessel. The ship had then righted itself and sailed on, drifting with the wind.

In the light of our beam the ship seemed

so sound, so strong, that Itchoua impatiently exclaimed, "But *why* was it abandoned? Nothing is smashed. There's no sign of fire. And it doesn't sail as if it were taking on water."

The three of us grew tense, for the ship seemed certain to crash on one of our reefs. But then it suddenly lurched with a change in the wind, and sailed away in the other direction.

"Bon voyage!" called Le Gleo to the departing ship. "It's leaving us, chief, and now we'll never know why—"

"No, it's not!" cried Itchoua, "It's turning! Look!"

As if obeying his words, the drifting ship slowly swung around and headed for us once more.

All through the night the vessel, moved by the currents and the wind, zigzagged near our lighthouse. Then suddenly the dawn broke, the sun rose, and it was day. The ship was plainly visible, and through our binoculars we could see its name in black letters on a white background:

Cornelius de Witt.

Just then a powerful wind came up, and the *Cornelius de Witt* headed straight toward us again. But this time it was too close to turn in time.

"Thunder!" cried Le Gleo. "It's going to smash on the reef! It's gone!"

I shook my head. "Yes—and we're helpless."

There was nothing we could do but watch. A ship sailing with all its sails spread as it runs before the wind, is one of the most beautiful sights in the world—but this time I could feel the tears stinging in my eyes as I saw this fine ship headed for its doom.

All this time our glasses were riveted on the ship. And then we suddenly cried out together:

"Rats!"

Now we knew why this ship—in perfect condition—was sailing without its crew aboard. They had been driven out by *rats*.

These were not those poor specimens of rats you see on shore, barely one foot long from their trembling noses to the tip of their skinny tails, wretched creatures that run and hide at the sound of a step.

No, these were ships' rats, huge, wise creatures, born on the sea, sailing all over the world, transferring from one ship to another. The rats of the sea are fierce, bold animals, large and strong. And they are intelligent and brave. If you so much as harm one, its sharp, loud cry will bring hordes of others to swarm over you—to tear at you and not cease, until your flesh has been stripped from the bones.

There is a well-known tale about these animals. A captain, thinking to protect his cargo, brought aboard his ship—not cats— but two terriers, dogs trained in the hunting, fighting, and killing of vicious rats. Within twenty-four hours the dogs were gone and never seen again. They had been overwhelmed, killed, and eaten by the rats.

At times, when the cargo is not sufficient, the rats attack the crew, either driving them from the ship or eating them alive. And now, looking closely at the *Cornelius de Witt*, I turned sick—for its lifeboats were still in place. It had *not* been abandoned!

On its deck, on its bridge, on every visible spot, was a mass of rats—a starving army of rats—on a vessel heading toward us!

There was a sharp crack as the ship hit the rock. There was a dull sound as the bottom smashed, then a horrible crackling as the three masts came crashing down and went overboard. Water rushed into the ship; then it split in two and sank like a stone.

But the rats did not drown. Not these fellows! As much at home in the sea as any fish, they formed ranks in the water, heads lifted, paws paddling. Before we had time even to move, nothing remained of the ship but some pieces of wreckage floating on the surface—and an army of rats that covered the rock as the tide went out.

Thousands of heads rose, felt the wind, and we were scented. *Seen!* To them we were fresh meat, after possible weeks of starving. There came a scream composed of thousands of screams, and in one motion every rat leaped to attack the lighthouse!

We had had barely time to jump back and close the door leading onto the gallery. Then we quickly descended the stairs and shut every window tightly. Luckily, the door at the base of the lighthouse was made of bronze set in granite and was firmly closed.

In no time at all the horrible band swarmed up and over the lighthouse as if it were a tree. The rats piled onto the ledges of the windows and scraped at the glass with thousands of claws. Their teeth grated as they pressed against the glass of the lantern room, where they could plainly see us, though they could not reach us. A half inch of glass, luckily very strong, separated our faces from their gleaming, beady eyes, their sharp claws and teeth. At the same time, their odor filled the tower and poisoned our lungs. So there we were, sealed alive in our own lighthouse— prisoners of a horde of starving rats!

That first night, the tension was so great that we could not sleep. Every moment we worried that some opening had been made, that some window had given way, and that

our horrible besiegers were pouring through. The rising tide forced some of the rats off the rocks, and they joined the others, clinging to the granite walls and ledges of the lighthouse.

When darkness came we turned on the light, and the rotating beam completely maddened the beasts. It blinded thousands of rats crowded against the glass, while the eyes of the others, gleaming with countless points of light, burned like the eyes of jungle beasts in the night.

All the while we could hear the angry scraping of claws against the stone and the glass. The chorus of cries was so deafening that we had to shout loudly to hear one another. From time to time, some of the rats fought among themselves and a dark cluster would slip off the wall, falling into the sea like ripe fruit from a tree. Then we would see streaks, as triangular fins slashed the water—sharks feasting on our jailers.

The next day we were calmer, and we amused ourselves by teasing the rats. We placed our faces against the glass that separated us. They could not understand the invisible barrier between us, and we laughed as we watched them leaping against the heavy glass. But the day after that, we realized how serious our situation was. The air was foul. And there was no way of letting in fresh air without also admitting the rats.

The morning of the fourth day, at early dawn, I saw that the wooden framework of my window had been eaten away from the outside and was sagging inward. I called my comrades and the three of us fastened a sheet of tin over the window, sealing it completely. When we had finished the task, Itchoua turned to us and said without emotion, "Well—the supply boat came thirteen days ago, so it won't be back for twenty-nine." He pointed at the sheet of tin over the window. "If that gives way," he shrugged, "they can change the name of this place to Six Skeleton Key."

Six days passed, during which our prison, the lighthouse, became even more gloomy. The light inside was by now almost completely dark, for we had to seal every window the same way we did mine. The only space that still admitted daylight was the glassed-in lantern room at the very top of the tower.

Then Le Gleo had nightmares in which he saw three skeletons dancing around him, gleaming coldly, as they tried to grasp him. His descriptions were so vivid that Itchoua and I began seeing them too.

It was a living nightmare, the shrieking cries of the rats as they swarmed over the lighthouse, mad with hunger, the sickening odor of their bodies—

There was only one thing left to do. After debating all of the ninth day, we decided not to turn on the light that night. This is the worst—the most terrible violation of our trust, for the light is something sacred, warning ships of danger in the night. It is understood that the light *must* go on fifteen minutes after sundown—unless there is no one in the lighthouse alive to light it.

Well, that night, Three Skeleton Light was dark—and all of us were alive! At the risk of causing ships to crash on the reef, we left the light unlit, for we were worn out—going mad!

At two in the morning, while Itchoua was dozing in his room, the sheet of metal sealing his window gave way. The chief had just time enough to leap to his feet and cry for help, the rats swarming in.

But Le Gleo and I, who had been on watch in the lantern room, got to him immediately.

The three of us battled furiously with the horde of maddened rats that flowed through the window. They bit, we struck them down again and again with our knives, then quickly we retreated.

We locked the door of the room on them, but before we had time to attend to our wounds, the door was eaten through and gave way. We rushed up the stairs, fighting off the rats that leaped on us from below.

I do not remember to this day how we ever managed to escape. All I can remember is wading through them up the stairs, striking them off as they swarmed over us. We pushed open the trapdoor above us and pulled ourselves up. Moments later we found ourselves bleeding, our clothes shredded, sprawled across the trapdoor in the floor of the lantern room. Luckily, the trapdoor was metal set into the granite. For the moment we were safe—but without food or drink.

The rats occupied the entire lighthouse beneath us. Below us, in the tower, we could hear the screams of the rats as they devoured everything that could possibly be eaten.

Itchoua sat up and stared silently at the blood trickling from the wounds on his limbs and body. Le Gleo, who was in a bad state, as was I, stared without expression at the chief and me. Then he suddenly began to laugh horribly. "Hee! Hee! The Three Skeletons are now *six* skeletons. *Six* skeletons! Hee! Hee!"

He threw his head back and howled. I shouted to him to shut up, but he did not seem to hear me. So I did the only thing I could to quiet him—I swung the back of my hand across his face.

The howling stopped suddenly. His eyes moved around the room, then he bowed his head and began weeping softly, like a child.

It had been noticed from the mainland that we had not lighted the lantern that night, and as dawn was breaking, the patrol was there to investigate the failure of our light. Looking through my binoculars, I could see the horrified expression on the faces of the crew when they saw the lighthouse completely covered by a seething mass of rats. They thought, I found out afterward, that we had been eaten alive.

But the rats had also seen the ship, or had scented the crew. As the ship drew nearer, a large pack of rats left the lighthouse, plunged into the water, and began swimming out, attempting to board it. They would have succeeded, too, for the ship was at drift, but the engineer quickly connected the steam pipe to a hose and fired a stream of scalding water at the attacking column. This slowed them up long enough for the ship to get under way, leaving the rats trailing behind.

But all this did nothing to get us out of our jail. The small ship could not approach directly but merely steamed around the lighthouse, a safe distance away. Meanwhile, the members of the crew, seeing the rats running in and out of the tower, decided we had perished. They were about to leave when Itchoua, regaining his senses, thought of using the light as a signal. He turned it on and, by covering and uncovering the light with a piece of wood, formed dots and dashes—a Morse code message that told our story.

The reply came shortly. A signalman, his arms swinging like a windmill, quickly spelled out:

"DON'T GIVE UP. HANG ON A LITTLE LONGER. WE'LL GET YOU OUT."

Then the ship turned and steamed at top speed for the coast. It was back at noon accompanied by the supply ship, a fireboat, and two coast guard patrol boats.

At twelve-thirty the battle was on. The fireboat carefully picked its way through the reefs until it was close to us. Then it turned its powerful jet of water on the rats. The heavy stream of water tore the rats from their places on the lighthouse and hurled them screaming into the water. But for every ten that were dislodged, seven made it back to the shore.

Nightfall came, and it was as if nothing had been done. The rats were still in possession. One of the patrol boats stayed by the island, while the other ships departed for the coast. We had to spend still another night in our prison. Le Gleo was sitting on the floor, babbling about skeletons. And as I turned to Itchoua, he fell unconscious from his wounds. I was in poor shape myself, and could feel I was running a fever.

Somehow the night dragged by, and the next afternoon I saw the fireboat returning from the mainland. It was accompanied by a tugboat pulling a huge barge. Through my glasses, I saw that the barge was filled with *meat*.

The tug, risking the treacherous reefs, dragged the barge as close to the island as possible. To the last rat, our besiegers deserted the rock and the lighthouse! They swam out and boarded the barge that reeked with the scent of freshly cut meat. The tug then dragged the barge about a mile from shore. There the fireboat drenched the barge with gasoline. Then a well-placed shell fired from the patrol boat set it on fire. The barge was immediately covered with a sheet of flames. The few rats that made it to the water were quickly disposed of by the sharks.

The patrol boat took us off the island, and by nightfall we were in a hospital on the mainland.

What became of my friends? Well, Le Gleo's mind cracked from the experience, and the doctors sent him back to France. There he spent the rest of his life in an institution, poor fellow. Itchoua died within a week. A rat's bite is dangerous in that hot, humid climate, and infection often sets in rapidly.

As for me—when they sprayed the lighthouse and repaired the damage done by the rats, I resumed my service there. Why not? I told you I liked the place. To be truthful, I've never had a post as pleasant as that one. And when my time finally came to depart from it forever, I was sorry to leave Three Skeleton Key.

Selecting details from the story.

The following questions help you check your reading comprehension. Put an *x* in the box next to each correct answer.

1. The narrator volunteered for service at Three Skeleton Key because
   - ☐ a. it was the only job he could find.
   - ☐ b. no one else was willing to work there.
   - ☐ c. the pay was high, and he wanted to save some money.

2. Eventually, the huge three-master ship
   - ☐ a. drifted out to sea and disappeared from view.
   - ☐ b. was towed to shore by the tugboat.
   - ☐ c. hit the rock and sank.

3. The lighthouse keepers decided to call attention to their desperate situation by
   - ☐ a. leaving the light off at night.
   - ☐ b. starting a large fire.
   - ☐ c. sending a radio message for help.

4. The rats finally left the lighthouse when they were
   - ☐ a. attacked by sharks.
   - ☐ b. lured away by the scent of freshly cut meat.
   - ☐ c. frightened off by the patrol boat.

Knowing new vocabulary words.

The following questions check your vocabulary skills. Put an *x* in the box next to each correct answer.

1. The engineer connected the steam pipe to a hose and fired a stream of scalding water at the rats. What is the meaning of the word *scalding*?
   - ☐ a. pleasing
   - ☐ b. burning
   - ☐ c. annoying

2. Large ships stayed a good distance away from the lighthouse because they could not maneuver easily among the reefs. Which expression best defines the word *maneuver*?
   - ☐ a. sink rapidly
   - ☐ b. destroy quickly
   - ☐ c. move skillfully

3. The men were afraid that some window would give way, permitting their besiegers to rush through. As used here, the word *besiegers* means
   - ☐ a. attackers.
   - ☐ b. diseases.
   - ☐ c. nightmares.

4. For every ten rats that were dislodged from the lighthouse and thrown into the sea, seven made it back to the rock. The word *dislodged* means
   - ☐ a. satisfied with.
   - ☐ b. forced out of.
   - ☐ c. attracted to.

	× 5 =	
NUMBER CORRECT		YOUR SCORE

	× 5 =	
NUMBER CORRECT		YOUR SCORE

IDENTIFYING STORY ELEMENTS. The following questions check your knowledge of story elements. Put an *x* in the box next to each correct answer.

1. What happened last in the *plot* of "Three Skeleton Key"?
   - ☐ a. A well-placed shell set the barge on fire.
   - ☐ b. Itchoua used the light to send a Morse code message.
   - ☐ c. The rats swarmed over the lighthouse and scraped at the windows.

2. Which sentence best *characterizes* the narrator of the story?
   - ☐ a. He was bored with the life at Three Skeleton Key and was eager to return home.
   - ☐ b. Despite a terrifying experience at Three Skeleton Key, he liked the place and was sorry to leave it.
   - ☐ c. He was so upset by the incident with the rats that he decided never to work at a lighthouse again.

3. What is the *setting* of "Three Skeleton Key"?
   - ☐ a. a lighthouse on an island of rock
   - ☐ b. a coast guard station in South Africa
   - ☐ c. a patrol boat somewhere at sea

4. Which word best describes the *mood* of the story?
   - ☐ a. humorous
   - ☐ b. horrifying
   - ☐ c. sorrowful

LOOKING AT CLOZE. The following questions use the cloze technique to check your reading comprehension. Complete the paragraph by filling in each blank with one of the words listed below. Each word appears in the story. Since there are five words and four blanks, one of the words will not be used.

How familiar are you with the terms that refer to the parts of a _____₁ ? Did you know that the front of the ship is called the *bow*, while the rear of the ship is _____₂ as the *stern*? The *hold* is the space where _____₃ is stored. The crow's nest, as the name suggests, is the lookout's platform, located a short _____₄ from the the top of the *mast*.

cargo   **separated**

ship

distance   **known**

	× 5 =	
NUMBER CORRECT		YOUR SCORE

	× 5 =	
NUMBER CORRECT		YOUR SCORE

LEARNING HOW TO READ CRITICALLY.
The following questions check your critical
thinking skills. Put an *x* in the box next to
each correct answer.

1. Clues in the story suggest that the crew
   of the *Cornelius de Witt*
   ☐ a. escaped to shore by using the ship's
      lifeboats.
   ☐ b. died in a fire aboard the ship.
   ☐ c. was devoured by rats.

2. When Le Gleo began to laugh horribly,
   the narrator struck him across the face.
   We may infer that the narrator did this
   because he
   ☐ a. wanted to bring Le Gleo back to his
      senses.
   ☐ b. was angry at Le Gleo.
   ☐ c. was a very violent person.

3. The author suggests that rats are
   ☐ a. actually timid and cowardly.
   ☐ b. less intelligent than people realize.
   ☐ c. capable of communicating with, and
      helping, one another.

4. Which statement is true?
   ☐ a. Itchoua recovered from his wounds
      and again took up service as a
      lighthouse keeper.
   ☐ b. The narrator appears to be a
      practical person who is somewhat
      of a loner.
   ☐ c. Le Gleo returned to France where
      he later wrote a book about
      lighthouses.

┌─────┐   ┌─────┐
│   │ × 5 =   │   │
└─────┘   └─────┘
 NUMBER   YOUR
 CORRECT   SCORE

Improving Writing and Discussion Skills

- "Three Skeleton Key" is probably a
  true story. Do you agree or disagree
  with this statement? Give reasons
  to support your answer.
- By deciding not to turn on the light,
  the men placed ships in the area in
  great danger. Keeping this in mind,
  do you think the men made the right
  decision? Should they have turned
  on the light, even if doing so added
  to their peril? Explain your point
  of view.
- It is obvious why "Three Skeleton Key"
  appears in a book called *Encounters*.
  Select *one* encounter from the story.
  Describe it briefly but vividly.

Use the boxes below to total your scores
for the exercises. Then write your score on
pages 140 and 141.

┌─────┐
│   │ SELECTING DETAILS FROM THE STORY
└─────┘
  +
┌─────┐
│   │ KNOWING NEW VOCABULARY WORDS
└─────┘
  +
┌─────┐
│   │ IDENTIFYING STORY ELEMENTS
└─────┘
  +
┌─────┐
│   │ LOOKING AT CLOZE
└─────┘
  +
┌─────┐
│   │ LEARNING HOW TO READ CRITICALLY
└─────┘
  ▼
┌─────┐
│   │ SCORE Total: Story 1
└─────┘

2. The Pimienta Pancakes

by O. Henry

Meet the Author

O. Henry (1862–1910) is the pen name of William Sidney Porter, a popular writer famous for short stories that feature his trademark surprise ending. Born in Greensboro, North Carolina, O. Henry eventually moved to New York City, the setting of many of his nearly 300 short stories. Some of O. Henry's best-known and loved works are collected in *The Four Million*. Other volumes include *Heart of the West*, *Roads of Destiny*, and *The Voice of the City*.

*W*hile we were rounding up a bunch of cattle on the Triangle-O ranch, I stepped into a gopher hole and wrenched my ankle so awful I couldn't work for a week.

On the third day of my forced idleness, I got to my knees and crawled out near the grub wagon where Judson Odom, the camp cook, was fixing up some provisions for supper. Jud was a born storyteller who usually lacked an audience, so I figured he'd be glad enough to have my company. Besides, I was suddenly overcome with the most terrible urge for a plate of pancakes.

"Jud," says I, "can you make me pancakes?"

Jud put down the sixshooter, with which he was preparing to pound an antelope steak. He stood over me in what I felt was a menacing manner. He further strengthened that impression by glaring at me with a look of cold suspicion.

19

"Say you," he said after a while, "did you really mean that, or was you just trying to get my goat? Some of the boys here been telling you about me and that pancake business?"

"No, Jud," I said, sincerely, "I meant it. It seems to me I'd swap my pony and saddle for a stack of buttered brown pancakes with maple syrup. Was there some kind of story about pancakes?"

When he saw that I was not poking fun, Jud relaxed at once. "No, not a story," said Jud as he worked, "just some facts in the case of me and that sheepman, Jackson Bird, and Miss Willella Learight. I'll tell you about it."

So I sat back in the shade and made myself comfortable while Jud told me the following:

"I was herding cattle for old Bill Toomey on Toomey's ranch," said Jud, "when I took it into my head that I needed to eat a bit of grub that had never mooed, or grunted, or baaed. So I gets on my bronc and heads over to Uncle Emsley Telfair's store over at Pimienta Crossing.

"When I got there it was about three in the afternoon. I sat down at the counter, and in no time at all, Uncle Emsley had served me up a batch of crackers and a big bowl of sliced apricots and pineapples. I was digging my spurs into the side of the counter and working away with my spoon, when I happened to look out the window into the yard of Uncle Emsley's house, which was next to the store.

"There was a young woman standing there, a stranger as far as I could tell. She seemed to be amusing herself by watching my style of devouring the fruit industry.

"I slid off the counter and inquired of Uncle Emsley.

" 'That's my niece,' says he. 'Miss Willella Learight down from back East on a visit. Do you want that I should make you acquainted?'

" 'Why yes, Uncle Emsley,' I says out loud. 'I'd be right proud to meet Miss Learight.'

"So Uncle Emsley took me out into the yard and introduced us to each other.

"I never was shy about women. I could never understand why some men who can lasso a bronco before breakfast and shave in the dark, get all full of perspiration and excuses when they're introduced to a lady. Inside of eight minutes, me and Miss Willella was as amiable as second cousins. She teased me about the quantity of canned fruit I had eaten. And I got back at her about how a certain lady named Eve had started the fruit trouble in the first place with the apple.

"That was how I first made the acquaintance of Miss Willella Learight. She was stopping at Pimienta Crossing to visit her uncle, and for the climate that was better than the climate back East. I rode over to see her once every week for a while. And then I figured out that if I doubled the number of trips I would see her twice as often.

"One week I slipped in a third trip—and that's where the pancakes and the sheepman figure into the story. While I was sitting at the counter with a peach in my mouth, I asked Uncle Emsley how Miss Willella was.

" 'Why,' says Uncle Emsley, 'she's gone riding with Jackson Bird, the sheepman over at the Lazy-O ranch.'

"I gulped hard and swallowed the peach pit. Then I walked out straight to where my bronc was tied.

" 'She's gone riding,' I whispered into my bronc's ear, 'with a sheepman. Do you hear that—a sheepman?'

"That bronc of mine looked at me in a

sad sort of way. He'd been raised a cow pony and he didn't care much for sheepmen.

"I went back and said to Uncle Emsley, 'Did you say a sheepman?'

" 'I said a sheepman,' says Uncle Emsley again. 'You must have heard tell of Jackson Bird. He's got eight sections of grazing land and four thousand head of the finest Merino sheep this side of Canada.'

"I went out and sat on the ground and sifted sand into my boots, while I thought about this bird with the Jackson feather to his name. I never had believed in harming sheepmen. They never irritated me like they do most cowmen. I saw one, one day, reading a Latin grammar book on hossback, and I never touched him. I had always let 'em pass, just as you would a jackrabbit. I always gave 'em a nod and a polite word about the weather. I never thought it was worthwhile to be hostile with a snoozer. And because I'd put up with 'em and let 'em be, here was one going around riding with Miss Willella Learight!

"An hour after sundown they came loping back, and stopped at Uncle Emsley's gate. The sheep person helped her off and they stood talking for a while. And then this Jackson Bird flies up into his saddle and trots off in the direction of his mutton ranch. By the time he got half a mile out of Pimienta, I rides up besides him on my bronc.

" 'Afternoon!' says I to him. 'You are now riding with a man who is commonly known as Dead-Certainty Judson—on account of the way that I shoot. When I get angry at a stranger and want him to know me, I always introduce myself before we draw, for I never did like to shake hands with a ghost.'

" 'Ah,' says he, just like that—'Ah, I'm glad to know you, Mr. Judson. I'm Jackson Bird from the Lazy-O ranch.'

"Just then one of my eyes saw a buzzard, and the other eye noticed a rabbit-hawk sitting in an elm. I popped 'em, one after the other, with my forty-five. 'Two out of two,' says I. 'Birds just naturally seem to draw my fire.'

" 'Nice shooting,' says the sheepman, without a flutter. 'But don't you ever miss? Mighty fine rain we had for the grass last week, Mr. Judson.'

" 'Listen,' says I, coming close, 'let's get down to particulars. That is a bad habit you have got of riding with young ladies over at Pimienta. I've known birds,' says I, 'to be served on toast for less than that. Miss Willella don't want any nest made out of sheep's wool by any bird of the Jacksonian clan. Now are you going to quit, or do you wish to gallop up against Dead-Certainty Judson?'

"Jackson Bird got a bit red, and then he laughed.

" 'Why, Mr. Judson,' says he, 'you've got the wrong idea. I've called on Miss Learight a few times, but not for the purpose you imagine. My object is purely a gastronomical[1] one.'

"I reached for my gun.

" 'Wait a minute,' says this Bird, 'till I explain. What would I do with a wife? If you ever saw that ranch of mine! Eating—that's all the pleasure I get out of sheep raising. Tell me, Mr. Judson, did you ever taste the pancakes that Miss Learight makes?'

" 'Me? No,' I told him. 'I never was advised she was anything special by way of a cook.'

" 'They're golden sunshine,' says he, 'honey-browned and delicious. I'd give two years of my life to get the recipe for making

---

1. **gastronomical:** having to do with the art of good eating.

them pancakes. That's what I went to see Miss Learight for. But I haven't been able to get it from her. It's an old recipe that's been in the family for seventy-five years. They hand it down from one generation to another, but they don't give it away to outsiders. If I could get that recipe so I could make them pancakes myself on my ranch, I'd be a happy man.'

" 'Are you sure,' I says to him, 'that it ain't the hand that mixes them pancakes you're after?'

" 'Sure,' says Jackson, 'Miss Learight is a mighty nice young lady, but I can assure you my intentions go no further than the desire to obtain a copy of the pancake recipe.'

" 'You ain't such a bad little man,' says I, trying to be fair. 'I was thinking some about making orphans of your sheep, but I'll let you fly away this time. But you stick to pancakes when it comes to Miss Learight, or there'll be singing at your ranch, and you won't be able to hear it.'

" 'To convince you that I am sincere,' says the sheepman, 'I'll ask you to help me. Miss Learight and you being closer friends, maybe she would do for you what she wouldn't for me. If you will get me a copy of that pancake recipe, I give you my word that I'll never call upon her again.'

" 'That's fair,' I says, and I shook hands with Jackson Bird. 'I'll get it for you if I can, and glad to oblige.' And he headed down the road to the Lazy-O, while I made my way back to Bill Toomey's ranch.

"It was five days later when I got another chance to ride over to Pimienta. Miss Willella and me passed a pleasant evening at Uncle Emsley's. She sang a bit and bothered the piano quite a lot with pieces from some operas. I gave imitations of a rattlesnake,

and told her about Snaky McFee's new way of skinning cows. Then I described the trip I made to St. Louis once. We were getting along in my estimation fine. Thinks I, if Jackson can be persuaded to bow out of the picture, I win. Then I recollect his promise about the pancake recipe, and I thinks I will coax it out of Miss Willella, and send Jackson Bird hopping on his way.

"So along about ten o'clock, I put on my best smile and says to Miss Willella, 'Now there's nothing in the world I like better than the taste of a nice hot pancake smothered in molasses.'

"Miss Willella gives a little jump on the piano stool and looks at me kind of strange.

" 'Yes,' says she, 'pancakes are real nice. Now what did you say was the name of that street in St. Louis where you lost your hat?'

" '*Pancake* Avenue,' I says, winking to show her that I knew about the family recipe, and wouldn't let her change the subject. 'Come on, now, Miss Willella,' I says, 'let's hear how you make 'em. Pancakes is just whirling in my head like wagon wheels. Start off the recipe now. What is it—pound of flour, six dozen eggs, and so on. How does the list of ingredients go?'

" 'Excuse me for a moment, please,' says Miss Willella. Then she gives me a quick kind of sideways look and slides off the piano stool. She goes off into the other room, and immediately Uncle Emsley comes in carrying a pitcher of water. He turns around to get a glass on the table, and I see a forty-five in his hip pocket. 'Great post-holes!' thinks I, 'these folks care so much about a family recipe, they protect it with firearms!'

" 'Drink this down here, now,' says Uncle Emsley, handing me the glass of water. 'You've rode too far today, Jud, and got yourself overexcited. Try not to think any more about pancakes.'

" 'Do you know how to make them pancakes, Uncle Emsley?' I asked.

" 'Well, I reckon you make 'em the usual way. Say, Jud, is Bill Toomey planning to ship beef to Kansas City again this spring?'

"That was all the pancake information I could get that night. I could see why Jackson Bird found it difficult work. So I dropped the subject and talked with Uncle Emsley for a while about hollow-horn cattle and cyclones. And then Miss Willella came in and said 'Goodnight,' and I hit the road for the ranch.

"About a week afterward I met Jackson Bird riding out of Pimienta as I rode in. We stopped on the road to exchange a few remarks.

" 'Got the recipe for them pancakes yet?' I asked him.

" 'Well, no,' says Jackson, 'I don't seem to have any success in getting hold of it. Did you try?'

" 'I did,' says I, 'and it was like trying to dig a well using a peanut shell. You'd think that pancake recipe was worth its weight in gold, the way they hold on to it.'

" 'I'm almost ready to give it up,' says Jackson, in a tone so discouraged I felt sorry for him. 'But I did want to know how to make them pancakes to eat on my lonely ranch,' he went on. 'I lie awake at nights thinking how good they are.'

" 'You keep on trying for it,' I tells him, 'and I'll do the same. One of us is bound to lasso that recipe before long. Well so long, Jacksy.'

"You see, by this time we was on the peacefullest of terms. When I saw that he wasn't after Miss Willella, I was able to

endure that snoozer. And in order to help out his appetite, I kept on trying to get that recipe from Miss Willella. But every time I said 'pancakes' she would get sort of nervous and try to change the subject. If I kept at it too long, she would slip out of the room and round up Uncle Emsley with his pitcher of water and his firearm.

"One day I galloped over to the store with a bunch of wild flowers that I had picked specially for Miss Willella. Uncle Emsley looked at 'em and says, 'Haven't ye heard the news?'

" 'What news?' I asks.

" 'Willella and Jackson Bird was married back East yesterday,' says he.

"I dropped them flowers in a cracker-barrel and waited a bit until my head stopped spinning.

" 'Would you mind saying that over again once more, Uncle Emsley?' says I. 'Maybe my hearing has gone wrong and that you only said that the price of cattle is rising, or something like that.'

" 'Married yesterday,' says Uncle Emsley, 'and gone to Niagara Falls on a honeymoon. Why, didn't you see none of the signs all along? Jackson Bird has been courting Willella ever since that day he took her out riding.'

" 'Then,' yells I, 'what was all that hogwash he gives me about pancakes? Tell me *that!*'

"When I said 'pancakes' Uncle Emsley sort of blinked and stepped back.

" 'Somebody's been dealing me pancakes from the bottom of the deck,' I says, 'and I believe you know it. Talk up!' says I.

"I hopped over the counter after Uncle Emsley. He grabbed for his gun, but it was in a drawer and he missed it by two inches. I grabbed him by the front of his shirt and shoved him into a corner.

" 'Talk pancakes,' says I, 'or be made into one! Does Miss Willella make 'em?'

" 'She never made one in her life,' says Uncle Emsley. 'Calm down now, Jud—calm down. You've got excited, and that wound in your head is bothering your brain. Try not to think about pancakes, now.'

" 'Uncle Emsley,' says I, 'I'm not wounded in the head! Jackson Bird told me he was calling on Miss Willella for the purpose of finding out her recipe for pancakes, and he asked me to help him. I done so with the results you see. Have I been sold a bill of goods by that wall-eyed snoozer, or what?'

" 'Loosen up your grip on my shirt,' says Uncle Emsley, 'and I'll tell you. Yes, it looks like Jackson Bird has gone and hornswoggled you some. The day after he went riding with Willella, he came back here and told me and her to watch out for you whenever you got to talking about pancakes. He said you was in camp once where they was making pancakes, and one of the fellows hit you over the head with a frying pan. Jackson said that whenever you got excited or upset that wound hurt you and made you kind of crazy, and you went raving about pancakes. He told us to just get you off the subject and soothe you down and you wouldn't be dangerous. So, me and Willella done the best we could.' "

During the course of his story, Jud had been slowly but surely combining various ingredients. Finally, he set before me the finished product—a batch of red-hot, golden-brown pancakes. He brought out a lump of butter and a bottle of syrup.

"How long ago did these things happen?" I asked.

"Three years," said Jud. "They're living on the Lazy-O ranch now, but I haven't seen either of 'em since. Oh, I got over it after a while. But the boys never stopped teasing me about them pancakes."

"Did you make these pancakes by the famous recipe?" I asked.

"Didn't I tell you there wasn't no recipe?" said Jud. "The boys kept hollering for pancakes, and finally I cut this recipe out of a newspaper. How do they taste?"

"They're delicious," I answered. "Why don't you have some?"

I was sure I heard a sigh.

"Me?" said Jud. "I don't never eat pancakes."

SELECTING DETAILS FROM THE STORY.
The following questions help you check your reading comprehension. Put an *x* in the box next to each correct answer.

1. Jackson Bird said that he was calling on Willella Learight for the purpose of
   □ a. asking for her hand in marriage.
   □ b. convincing her to write a cookbook.
   □ c. obtaining the family recipe for pancakes.

2. When Judson Odom mentioned pancakes to Willella, she
   □ a. felt flattered.
   □ b. grew nervous.
   □ c. laughed loudly.

3. Uncle Emsley told Jud that Jackson Bird had
   □ a. never really been interested in Willella.
   □ b. been courting Willella since the day they went riding.
   □ c. sold his ranch and was moving to Canada.

4. At the end of the story, Jud made pancakes by using a recipe that
   □ a. Willella mailed to him.
   □ b. one of the ranchers gave him.
   □ c. he cut out of a newspaper.

KNOWING NEW VOCABULARY WORDS.
The following questions check your vocabulary skills. Put an *x* in the box next to each correct answer.

1. In Jud's estimation, he and Willella had been getting along fine. As used here, the word *estimation* means
   □ a. opinion or judgment.
   □ b. confusion or bewilderment.
   □ c. skill or ability.

2. Although Jud didn't like sheepmen, they didn't irritate him as much as they did most cowmen. Which of the following best defines the word *irritate*?
   □ a. assist
   □ b. annoy
   □ c. welcome

3. Jud wasn't shy with women; minutes after he and Willella met, they were amiable as second cousins. The word *amiable* means
   □ a. friendly.
   □ b. uncomfortable.
   □ c. thoughtless.

4. Five days later, Jud began to recollect the promise that Jackson had made. What is the meaning of the word *recollect*?
   □ a. attack
   □ b. break
   □ c. remember

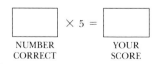

NUMBER CORRECT	× 5 =	YOUR SCORE

NUMBER CORRECT	× 5 =	YOUR SCORE

IDENTIFYING STORY ELEMENTS. The following questions check your knowledge of story elements. Put an *x* in the box next to each correct answer.

1. Where is "The Pimienta Pancakes" *set?*
   □ a. in a large city in the North
   □ b. somewhere in the East
   □ c. in the West

2. What happened first in the *plot* of the story?
   □ a. Jud grabbed Uncle Emsley and shoved him into a corner.
   □ b. Willella saw Jud devouring fruit at the counter.
   □ c. Jackson Bird asked Jud to help him get a recipe.

3. Judging by "The Pimienta Pancakes," what is true of O. Henry's *style* of writing?
   □ a. His stories contain numerous passages that are highly poetic.
   □ b. His stories do not contain any dialogue.
   □ c. His stories conclude with a surprise.

4. What was the author's *purpose* in writing the story?
   □ a. to entertain or amuse the reader
   □ b. to frighten or scare the reader
   □ c. to teach the reader a very valuable lesson

LOOKING AT CLOZE. The following questions use the cloze technique to check your reading comprehension. Complete the paragraph by filling in each blank with one of the words listed below. Each word appears in the story. Since there are five words and four blanks, one of the words will not be used.

You may be surprised to learn that there are hundreds of different kinds of

_____. One popular variety

is _____ Viennese cheese pan-
      2

cakes. Eggs, flour, and milk are the main

_____. In this recipe, the
      3

pancakes are fried. Then they are wrapped

_____ pot cheese and raisins
      4

and are baked.

around   audience

pancakes

ingredients   called

<table>
<tr><td>□</td><td>× 5 =</td><td>□</td></tr>
<tr><td>NUMBER
CORRECT</td><td></td><td>YOUR
SCORE</td></tr>
</table>

<table>
<tr><td>□</td><td>× 5 =</td><td>□</td></tr>
<tr><td>NUMBER
CORRECT</td><td></td><td>YOUR
SCORE</td></tr>
</table>

LEARNING HOW TO READ CRITICALLY.
The following questions check your critical
thinking skills. Put an *x* in the box next to
each correct answer.

1. Jud wanted to eat something "that had
   never mooed, or grunted, or baaed." By
   this Jud meant that he wanted to eat
   ☐ a. some hamburgers.
   ☐ b. a batch of pancakes.
   ☐ c. something other than meat.

2. When he learned that Jackson and Willella
   had gotten married, Jud was
   ☐ a. not particularly surprised.
   ☐ b. shocked and amazed.
   ☐ c. happy for the couple.

3. Clues in the story suggest that Willella
   ☐ a. was deeply in love with Jud.
   ☐ b. was fascinated by Jud and his
       amazing stories.
   ☐ c. wasn't seriously interested in Jud
       but simply acted courteously to him.

4. Based on what happened in the story,
   it is reasonable to conclude that Jud
   ☐ a. was not as smart as he thought
       he was.
   ☐ b. didn't really care about Willella.
   ☐ c. had been injured by a frying pan
       in a fight years ago.

Improving Writing and Discussion Skills

- The name "Jackson *Bird*" is the source
  of much humor in the story. Find as
  many examples as you can to illus-
  trate this point.
- Why did Uncle Emsley offer Jud some
  water whenever he began to talk about
  pancakes? Do you think this should
  have made Jud suspicious? Why?
- "The Pimienta Pancakes" is an
  obvious title for the story. Think of
  another name that would also be
  appropriate. Make it humorous, if
  possible.

Use the boxes below to total your scores
for the exercises. Then write your score on
pages 140 and 141.

☐
  +
Sᴇʟᴇᴄᴛɪɴɢ ᴅᴇᴛᴀɪʟs ғʀᴏᴍ ᴛʜᴇ sᴛᴏʀʏ

☐
  +
Kɴᴏᴡɪɴɢ ɴᴇᴡ ᴠᴏᴄᴀʙᴜʟᴀʀʏ ᴡᴏʀᴅs

☐
  +
Iᴅᴇɴᴛɪғʏɪɴɢ sᴛᴏʀʏ ᴇʟᴇᴍᴇɴᴛs

☐
  +
Lᴏᴏᴋɪɴɢ ᴀᴛ ᴄʟᴏᴢᴇ

☐
  ▼
Lᴇᴀʀɴɪɴɢ ʜᴏᴡ ᴛᴏ ʀᴇᴀᴅ ᴄʀɪᴛɪᴄᴀʟʟʏ

☐
Sᴄᴏʀᴇ Total: Story 2

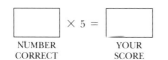

	× 5 =	
NUMBER CORRECT		YOUR SCORE

3. The Marble Champ

by Gary Soto

Meet the Author

Gary Soto (1952–   ) is an award-winning poet
and children's book author. Born in Fresno,
California, he is currently associate professor of
Chicano Studies and English at the University
of California at Berkeley. Soto's collection of
short stories, *Baseball in April,* was named an
ALA Best Book for Young Adults. His other
works include *Living up the Street,* a collection
of autobiographical essays, *Pacific Crossing,* a
novel, and *Neighborhood Odes,* a book of poems.

*L*upe Medrano, a shy girl who spoke
in whispers, was the school's spelling bee
champion, winner of the reading contest at
the public library three summers in a row,
blue ribbon awardee in the science fair, the
top student at her piano recital, and the playground grand champion in chess. She was
a straight-A student and—not counting kindergarten, when she had been stung by a wasp—
never missed one day of elementary school.
She had received a small trophy for this honor
and had been congratulated by the mayor.

But though Lupe had a razor-sharp mind,
she could not make her body, no matter how
much she tried, run as fast as the other girls'.
She begged her body to move faster, but could
never beat anyone in the fifty-yard dash.

The truth was that Lupe was no good in
sports. She could not catch a pop-up or figure
out in which direction to kick the soccer ball.

One time she kicked the ball at her own goal and scored a point for the other team. She was no good at baseball or basketball either, and even had a hard time making a hula hoop stay on her hips.

It wasn't until last year, when she was eleven years old, that she learned how to ride a bike. And even then she had to use training wheels. She could walk in the swimming pool but couldn't swim, and chanced roller skating only when her father held her hand.

"I'll never be good at sports," she fumed one rainy day as she lay on her bed gazing at the shelf her father had made to hold her awards. "I wish I could win something, anything, even marbles."

At the word "marbles," she sat up. "That's it. Maybe I could be good at playing marbles." She hopped out of bed and rummaged through the closet until she found a can full of her brother's marbles. She poured the rich glass treasure on her bed and picked five of the most beautiful marbles.

She smoothed her bedspread and practiced shooting, softly at first so that her aim would be accurate. The marble rolled from her thumb and clicked against the targeted marble. But the target wouldn't budge. She tried again and again. Her aim became accurate, but the power from her thumb made the marble move only an inch or two. Then she realized that the bedspread was slowing the marbles. She also had to admit that her thumb was weaker than the neck of a newborn chick.

She looked out the window. The rain was letting up, but the ground was too muddy to play. She sat cross-legged on the bed, rolling her five marbles between the palms. Yes, she thought, I could play marbles, and marbles is a sport. At that moment she realized that

she had only two weeks to practice. The playground championship, the same one her brother had entered the previous year, was coming up. She had a lot to do.

To strengthen her wrists, she decided to do twenty push-ups on her fingertips, five at a time. "One, two, three . . ." she groaned. By the end of the first set she was breathing hard, and her muscles burned from exhaustion. She did one more set and decided that was enough push-ups for the first day.

She squeezed a rubber eraser one hundred times, hoping it would strengthen her thumb. This seemed to work because the next day her thumb was sore. She could hardly hold a marble in her hand, let alone send it flying with power. So Lupe rested that day and listened to her brother, who gave her tips on how to shoot: get low, aim with one eye, and place one knuckle on the ground.

"Think 'eye and thumb'—and let it rip!" he said.

After school the next day she left her homework in her backpack and practiced three hours straight, taking time only to eat a candy bar for energy. With a popsicle stick, she drew an odd-shaped circle and tossed in four marbles. She used her shooter, a milky agate with hypnotic swirls, to blast them. Her thumb *had* become stronger.

After practice, she squeezed the eraser for an hour. She ate dinner with her left hand to spare her shooting hand and said nothing to her parents about her dreams of athletic glory.

Practice, practice, practice. Squeeze, squeeze, squeeze. Lupe got better and beat her brother and Alfonso, a neighbor kid who was supposed to be a champ.

"Man, she's bad!" Alfonso said. "She can beat the other girls for sure. I think."

The weeks passed quickly. Lupe worked so hard that one day, while she was drying dishes, her mother asked why her thumb was swollen.

"It's muscle," Lupe explained. "I've been practicing for the marbles championship."

"You, honey?" Her mother knew Lupe was no good at sports.

"Yeah. I beat Alfonso, and he's pretty good."

That night, over dinner, Mrs. Medrano said, "Honey, you should see Lupe's thumb."

"Huh?" Mr. Medrano said, wiping his mouth and looking at his daughter.

"Show your father."

"Do I have to?" an embarrassed Lupe asked.

"Go on, show your father."

Reluctantly, Lupe raised her hand and flexed her thumb. You could see the muscle.

The father put down his fork and asked, "What happened?"

"Dad, I've been working out. I've been squeezing an eraser."

"Why?"

"I'm going to enter the marbles championship."

Her father looked at her mother and then back at his daughter. "When is it, honey?"

"This Saturday. Can you come?"

The father had been planning to play racquetball with a friend Saturday, but he said he would be there. He knew his daughter thought she was no good at sports and he wanted to encourage her. He even rigged some lights in the backyard so she could practice after dark. He squatted with one knee on the ground, entranced by the sight of his daughter easily beating her brother.

The day of the championship began with a cold blustery sky. The sun was a silvery light behind slate clouds.

"I hope it clears up," her father said, rubbing his hands together as he returned from getting the newspaper. They ate breakfast, paced nervously around the house waiting for 10:00 to arrive, and walked the two blocks to the playground (though Mr. Medrano wanted to drive so Lupe wouldn't get tired). She signed up and was assigned her first match on baseball diamond number three.

Lupe, walking between her brother and her father, shook from the cold, not nerves. She took off her mittens, and everyone stared at her thumb. Someone asked, "How can you play with a broken thumb?" Lupe smiled and said nothing.

She beat her first opponent easily, and felt sorry for the girl because she didn't have anyone to cheer for her. Except for her sack of marbles, she was all alone. Lupe invited the girl, whose name was Rachel, to stay with them. She smiled and said, "OK." The four of them walked to a card table in the middle of the outfield, where Lupe was assigned another opponent.

She also beat this girl, a fifth-grader named Yolanda, and asked her to join their group. They proceeded to more matches and more wins, and soon there was a crowd of people following Lupe to the finals to play a girl in a baseball cap. The girl seemed dead serious. She never even looked at Lupe.

"I don't know, Dad, she looks tough."

Rachel hugged Lupe and said, "Go get her."

"You can do it," her father encouraged. "Just think of the marbles, not the girl, and let your thumb do the work."

The other girl broke first and earned one marble. She missed her next shot, and Lupe, one eye closed, her thumb quivering with energy, blasted two marbles out of the circle but missed her next shot. Her opponent earned two more before missing. She stamped her foot and said "Shoot!" The score was three to two in favor of Miss Baseball Cap.

The referee stopped the game. "Back up, please, give them room," he shouted. Onlookers had gathered too tightly around the players.

Lupe then earned three marbles and was set to get her fourth when a gust of wind blew dust in her eyes and she missed badly. Her opponent quickly scored two marbles, tying the game, and moved ahead six to five on a lucky shot. Then she missed, and Lupe, whose eyes felt scratchy when she blinked, relied on instinct and thumb muscle to score the tying point. It was now six to six, with only three marbles left. Lupe blew her nose and studied the angles. She dropped to one knee, steadied her hand, and shot so hard she cracked two marbles from the circle. She was the winner!

"I did it!" Lupe said under her breath. She rose from her knees, which hurt from bending all day, and hugged her father. He hugged her back and smiled.

Everyone clapped, except Miss Baseball Cap, who made a face and stared at the ground. Lupe told her she was a great player, and they shook hands. A newspaper photographer took pictures of the two girls standing shoulder-to-shoulder, with Lupe holding the bigger trophy.

Lupe then played the winner of the boys' division, and after a poor start beat him eleven to four. She blasted the marbles, shattering one into sparkling slivers of glass. Her opponent looked on glumly as Lupe did what she did best—win!

The head referee and the President of the Fresno Marble Association stood with Lupe as she displayed her trophies for the newspaper photographer. Lupe shook hands with everyone, including a dog who had come over to see what the commotion was all about.

That night, the family went out for pizza and set the two trophies on the table for everyone in the restaurant to see. People came up to congratulate Lupe, and she felt a little embarrassed, but her father said the trophies belonged there.

Back home, in the privacy of her bedroom, she placed the trophies on her shelf and was happy. She had always earned honors because of her brains, but winning in sports was a new experience. She thanked her tired thumb. "You did it, thumb. You made me champion." As its reward, Lupe went to the bathroom, filled the bathroom sink with warm water, and let her thumb swim and splash as it pleased. Then she climbed into bed and drifted into a hard-won sleep.

SELECTING DETAILS FROM THE STORY. The following questions help you check your reading comprehension. Put an *x* in the box next to each correct answer.

1. To strengthen her thumb, Lupe
   ☐ a. squeezed an eraser.
   ☐ b. bathed it in warm water.
   ☐ c. rested it as much as possible.

2. When Mr. Medrano learned that his daughter would be in the marbles championship, he
   ☐ a. said that he couldn't attend because he was playing racquetball that day.
   ☐ b. didn't believe that she was telling him the truth.
   ☐ c. said that he would be there.

3. What tip did Lupe's brother give her for shooting marbles?
   ☐ a. Try to upset your opponents by staring at them and looking tough.
   ☐ b. Keep both eyes on the marble, and fire as hard as you can all the time.
   ☐ c. Get low, aim with one eye, and keep one knuckle on the ground.

4. When people congratulated Lupe in the restaurant, she
   ☐ a. boasted about how good she was.
   ☐ b. felt a little embarrassed.
   ☐ c. said that she didn't really deserve to win.

KNOWING NEW VOCABULARY WORDS. The following questions check your vocabulary skills. Put an *x* in the box next to each correct answer.

1. "Do I have to?" an embarrassed Lupe asked reluctantly. The word *reluctantly* means
   ☐ a. eagerly.
   ☐ b. pleasantly.
   ☐ c. unwillingly.

2. Lupe blasted the marbles, shattering one into sparkling slivers of glass. What are *slivers*?
   ☐ a. thin, sharp pieces
   ☐ b. large, solid objects
   ☐ c. heavy pieces of plastic

3. The father was entranced by the sight of his daughter winning so easily. What is the meaning of the word *entranced*?
   ☐ a. delighted
   ☐ b. bothered
   ☐ c. warned

4. When Lupe flexed her thumb, you could see the muscle. Which of the following best defines the word *flexed*?
   ☐ a. broke
   ☐ b. bent
   ☐ c. washed

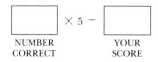

× 5 =

NUMBER
CORRECT

YOUR
SCORE

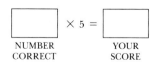

× 5 =

NUMBER
CORRECT

YOUR
SCORE

IDENTIFYING STORY ELEMENTS. The following questions check your knowledge of story elements. Put an x in the box next to each correct answer.

1. Who is the *main character* in "The Marble Champ"?
   - ☐ a. Mr. Medrano
   - ☐ b. Lupe
   - ☐ c. Rachel

2. What happened last in the *plot* of the story?
   - ☐ a. The referee stopped the game and asked the onlookers to move back.
   - ☐ b. Lupe beat Alfonso, who was supposed to be a champ.
   - ☐ c. In the privacy of her bedroom, Lupe placed the trophies on her shelf.

3. What was Lupe's *motive* for entering the marbles competition?
   - ☐ a. She wanted to win something— anything, in sports.
   - ☐ b. She hoped that winning would make her more popular at school.
   - ☐ c. Her family forced her to sign up.

4. Which sentence best expresses the *theme* of the story?
   - ☐ a. If you are really good at something, it is not necessary to put much effort into it to succeed.
   - ☐ b. A star athlete easily wins a marbles championship.
   - ☐ c. Through determination and practice, a girl who has never done well in athletics becomes a marbles champion.

☐ × 5 = ☐

NUMBER CORRECT   YOUR SCORE

LOOKING AT CLOZE. The following questions use the cloze technique to check your reading comprehension. Complete the paragraph by filling in each blank with one of the words listed below. Each word appears in the story. Since there are five words and four blanks, one of the words will not be used.

Just as _____ players have
                     1
their favorite bat, marbles players have their

favorite marble. This is usually the shooter—

the one the player uses to attack the

opponents' _____ . Since most
                        2
marbles are made of _____ ,
                                3
every now and then a shooter chips.

When that happens, the unhappy

_____ is forced to find another
          4
favorite marble.

marbles   **glass**

trophy

player   **baseball**

☐ × 5 = ☐

NUMBER CORRECT   YOUR SCORE

LEARNING HOW TO READ CRITICALLY.
The following questions check your critical
thinking skills. Put an *x* in the box next to
each correct answer.

1. Probably, people thought that Lupe's
   thumb was broken because
   - ☐ a. she complained about how much
     it hurt her.
   - ☐ b. it appeared to be swollen.
   - ☐ c. she could hardly move it.

2. Alfonso said of Lupe, "Man, she's bad!"
   By this he meant that she was
   - ☐ a. a terrible player.
   - ☐ b. a poor sport.
   - ☐ c. very good.

3. Which statement is true?
   - ☐ a. Although Lupe studied very hard,
     her grades were just average.
   - ☐ b. Lupe was one of the fastest runners
     in her class.
   - ☐ c. Until Lupe won the marbles
     championship, she had never
     finished first in any sport.

4. We may infer that if Lupe had lost the
   championship, she would have
   - ☐ a. accepted defeat graciously.
   - ☐ b. complained about the referee.
   - ☐ c. argued with the winner.

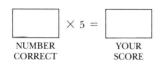

NUMBER   YOUR
CORRECT   SCORE

Improving Writing and Discussion Skills

- Suppose that Lupe had not won the
  marbles championship but had come
  in second. How disappointed do you
  think she would have been? Give
  reasons to support your opinion.
- Lupe is described as "a shy girl who
  spoke in whispers." Do you think that
  the experience of participating in, and
  winning, the championship will make
  Lupe less shy? Now that she has won
  the championship, do you think Lupe
  will compete in other athletic events?
  Will she enter the marbles championship next year? Explain your answers.
- Sometimes a story offers a lesson,
  or moral. What lessons can be drawn
  from "The Marble Champ"? Present
  at least two.

Use the boxes below to total your scores
for the exercises. Then write your score on
pages 140 and 141.

SELECTING DETAILS FROM THE STORY

+

KNOWING NEW VOCABULARY WORDS

+

IDENTIFYING STORY ELEMENTS

+

LOOKING AT CLOZE

+

LEARNING HOW TO READ CRITICALLY

▼

Score Total: Story 3

4. **Phut Phat Concentrates**

by Lilian Jackson Braun

*P*hut Phat knew, at an early age, that human beings were inferior to cats. Humans were unable to see in the dark. They ate and drank things which tasted terrible. And humans had only five senses. The two who lived with Phut Phat, the cat, could communicate their thoughts only by using words.

For more than a year—ever since arriving at the brownstone—Phut Phat had been trying to introduce *his* system of communication. But his two pupils had made little progress. At dinnertime he would sit in a corner, *concentrating*, thinking deeply. And then suddenly they would say, "It's time to feed the cat," as if it were *their* idea.

Their ability to receive Phut Phat's messages was very limited, however. Most messages never got through to them, unfortunately. Still, life in the brownstone was comfortable enough. There was a pleasant routine, meals were seldom tardy, and Phut Phat always had liver on Sunday.

Meet the Author

Lilian Jackson Braun (1916–   ) is famous for her stories and novels featuring cats. In 1966 she wrote her first "Cat Who" mystery, *The Cat Who Could Read Backwards.* Since then she has written more than a dozen books in the series, many of them best sellers. Fourteen of Braun's stories, including "Phut Phat Concentrates," are collected in *The Cat Who Had 14 Tales.*

It was a fashionable part of the city in which Phut Phat lived. The three-story brick brownstone was furnished with thick rugs and tall pieces of furniture from which he could look down on questionable visitors. When he scampered from the first-floor kitchen, to the second-floor living room, up to the third-floor bedroom, his flight was very swift, for Phut Phat was a Siamese. His coat was extremely fine and was sleek as velvet, and his slanted eyes glistened with a mysterious blue.

The humans who lived with Phut Phat were identified in his mind as One and Two. It was One who fed him and paid him many compliments. Two, on the other hand, was valued chiefly for entertainment. He said very little, but he jingled keys at the end of a shiny chain and swung them back and forth for Phut Phat's amusement. And every morning, in the dressing room, he swished a necktie in wide arcs, while Phut Phat leaped and grabbed at it with his paws.

Phut Phat's life consisted mainly of some daily frolics through the house, naps on soft cushions, outings to his large wire cage on the fire escape, and two meals a day.

Then one Sunday Phut Phat sensed a disturbing change in the household routine. Usually the Sunday papers were scattered on the floor for him to shred, but this day they were stacked neatly on the desk. Furniture was rearranged. One was nervous, and Two was too busy to play. The house was filled with flowers, which he was not allowed to chew. A stranger in a white coat arrived and set up plates and glasses. And when Phut Phat went into the kitchen to investigate the aroma of shrimp and smoked oysters, he was shooed away.

Phut Phat seemed to be in everyone's way.

Finally, he was placed in his cage on the fire escape, where he watched birds in the garden below until his stomach felt empty. Then he howled to come inside.

He found One busy at her dressing table. She had forgotten to feed him. He hopped lightly onto the table and fastened his blue eyes on One's forehead. Then he proceeded to concentrate—and concentrate—and *concentrate*. It was never easy to communicate with One. Her mind hopped around like a sparrow; it never relaxed. So Phut Phat had to strain every nerve to convey his meaning.

But then, suddenly, One darted a look in his direction. The thought had come into her mind!

"Oh, John," she called to Two, who was brushing his teeth, "would you feed Phuffy? I forgot his dinner until this very minute. It's after five o'clock and I haven't fixed my hair yet. You might put on some music, too. The guests will start arriving soon. Just give Phuffy a can of anything."

At this, Phut Phat stared at One's forehead and concentrated fiercely.

"Oh, John, I forgot," she corrected. "It's Sunday, and he'll expect liver."

Phut Phat hardly had time to finish his meal and wash his face before people started to arrive. Although he was annoyed by the change in routine, he was pleased at the idea of being admired by the guests. His name meant "beautiful" in Siamese, and he was beautiful, indeed. He lounged between a pair of tall silver candlesticks and waited for compliments.

It was a large party, and Phut Phat observed that very few of the guests knew how to pay their respects to a cat. Some talked nonsense in a false voice. Others moved suddenly in his direction or, worse still, tried to pick him up.

There was one man, however, who approached with exactly the right attitude. Phut Phat squeezed his eyes in admiration. This man was very distinguished-looking, and leaned heavily on a shiny silver stick. He stood at a respectful distance and slowly held out his hand with one finger extended. Phut Phat twitched his whiskers politely.

"You are a living sculpture," said the man.

"That's Phut Phat," said One, who had pushed through the crowded room toward the fireplace. "He's really the head of our household."

"He is obviously an exceptionally fine cat," said the man with the shiny cane. He addressed his hostess in the same dignified manner that had charmed Phut Phat.

"Yes, he could probably win ribbons if we wanted to enter him in shows. But he's strictly a pet. He never goes out except in his cage on the fire escape."

"A splendid idea!" said the guest. "I should like to set up an arrangement like that for my own cat. May I inspect his cage before I leave?"

"Certainly, it's just outside the window. I'll be glad to show it to you."

"You have a most attractive house."

"Thank you."

"Indeed, I have noticed that you collect old silver," the man said. "You have some fine examples."

"Apparently you know silver. Your cane is a rare piece."

"Yes," said the man, as he hobbled a step or two.

"Would you like to see my silver collection downstairs in the dining room?" asked One. "There are some wonderful examples."

Phut Phat became aware that the conversation no longer centered on him. Annoyed, he jumped down from the mantel and stalked out of the room with several irritable flicks of his tail. Then he went upstairs to the guest room where he went to sleep.

After this upset in the household routine, Phut Phat needed several days to catch up on his rest, so the rest of the week was a sleepy blur. But soon it was Sunday again, with liver for breakfast, Sunday papers scattered around the room, and everyone lounging around pleasantly.

"By the way, dear," said One, "who was that charming man with the silver cane at our party? I didn't catch his name."

"I don't know," said Two. "I thought he was someone you invited."

"Well, he must have come with one of the other guests. At any rate, he was interested in getting a cage like ours for his cat. Speaking of cats, did I tell you the Hendersons just got two Burmese kittens? They want us to go over there next Sunday and see them."

Another week passed, a routine week, followed by a routine weekend, and Phut Phat was content. One and Two were going out that Sunday evening to see the Burmese kittens, so Phut Phat was served an early dinner, after which he fell asleep on the sofa.

When the telephone rang and awakened him, it was dark and he was alone. He raised his head and stared at the telephone until it stopped its noise. Then he went back to sleep, chin on paw.

The second time the telephone started ringing, Phut Phat stood up and scolded it, arching his body and making a question mark with his tail. Then he spent a long time chewing on a leather bookmark.

Suddenly, something caused him to raise his head and listen. His tail froze. Sparrows in the backyard? Rain on the fire escape? There was silence again.

Phut Phat listened carefully. Nothing escaped his attention. Something was happening that was not routine. His tail bushed like a squirrel's, and with his whiskers full of alarm, he stepped noiselessly into the hall.

Someone was on the fire escape. Something was tapping at the window.

Petrified, he watched—until the window opened and a dim figure slipped into the room. With one lightning glide, Phut Phat sprang to the top of a tall dresser.

There, on his high perch, able to look down on the scene, he felt safe. But was it enough to feel safe? Centuries ago, his ancestors had been watch-cats in Oriental temples. They had hidden in the shadows and crouched on high walls, ready to spring on any intruder and tear at his face.

The figure in the window advanced slowly and stealthily toward the hall. Then Phut Phat experienced a sense of the familiar. It was the man with the shiny stick. This time, though, his presence smelled evil and sinister. A small blue light now glowed from the head of the cane, and instead of leaning on it, the man pointed it ahead of him to guide his way. As the man passed the tall dresser, Phut Phat's fur rose. Instinct said, "Spring at him!" But vague fears held him back.

Quietly, the man moved downstairs, unaware of two flowing diamond eyes that watched him in the blackness. Soon Phut Phat heard noises in the dining room. He sensed evil again. Safe on top of the dresser, he trembled.

When the man appeared once more, he was carrying a bulky load, which he took to the window. Then he moved on to the third floor. Phut Phat licked his nose in apprehension.

Now the man appeared again, following the line of blue light. As he approached the dresser, Phut Phat shifted his feet and braced himself. He felt a powerful urge to attack and, at the same time, a fearful dismay.

"Get him!" something powerful within him commanded.

"Stay!" warned the fright throbbing in his head.

"Get him! . . . Now. . . . Now. . . . . . *NOW!*

Phut Phat sprang at the man, ripping at him with his sharp claws wherever they sank into flesh.

The hideous scream that came from the man was like an electric shock. It sent Phut Phat sailing through space—up the stairs—into the bedroom—under the bed.

For a long time, Phut Phat quaked uncontrollably. His mouth was parched, and his ears were inside out with horror at what had happened. There was something strange and wrong about it, although he could not quite figure out its meaning. Waiting for time to heal his confusion, he huddled there in the darkness.

When One and Two came home, he sensed their arrival even before the taxi door slammed. He should have bounded out to meet them, but the experience had left him in a daze. He found himself quivering, weak and unsure. He heard the rattle of the front door lock. Then he heard feet climbing the stairs, and the click of the light switch in the room where he waited in bewilderment under the bed.

One gasped, then cried out. "John! Someone's been in this room. We've been robbed!"

Two's voice was shocked. "How do you know?"

"My jewel case! Look! It's open—and empty!"

"Helen. What about money? Did you have any money in the house?"

"I never leave money around. But the silver! What about the silver? John, go and see. I'm afraid to look . . . No! Wait a minute!" One's voice rose with panic. "Where's Phut Phat? What happened to Phut Phat?"

"I don't know," said Two with alarm. "I haven't seen him since we came in."

They searched the house, calling his name—unaware, with their limited senses, that Phut Phat was right there under the bed, brooding over what had happened, and now and then licking his claws.

When at last, crawling on their hands and knees, they spied two eyes glowing under the bed, they drew him out gently. One hugged him with a rocking embrace and rubbed her face, which was wet and salty, on his fur, while Two stood by, stroking him softly. Comforted and reassured, Phut Phat stopped trembling. He tried to purr but found it difficult to do so.

One continued to hold Phut Phat in her arms. He didn't even jump down after two strange men were admitted to the house. They asked questions and examined all the rooms.

"Everything is insured," One told them. "But it would be impossible to replace the silver. It's old and very rare. Is there any chance of getting it back, Lieutenant?" She stroked Phut Phat's ears nervously.

"At this point it's hard to say," the detective said, "but you may be able to help us. Have you noticed any strange incidents lately? Any unusual telephone calls?"

"Yes," said One. "Several times recently the phone has rung, and when we answered it, no one was there."

"That's the usual method. They wait until you're not at home."

One gazed into Phut Phat's eyes. "Did the phone ring tonight while we were out, Phuffy?" she asked, shaking him lovingly. "If only Phut Phat could tell us what happened! He must have had a terrifying experience. Thankfully, he wasn't harmed."

Phut Phat raised his paws.

"If only Phut Phat could tell us who was here!"

Phut Phat paused. He stared at One's forehead.

"Have you folks noticed any strangers in the neighborhood?" the lieutenant was asking. "Anyone suspicious?"

Phut Phat's body tensed, and his blue eyes, brimming with knowledge, stared hard at One's forehead.

"I can't think of anyone. Can you, John?"

Two shook his head.

"Poor Phuffy," said One. "See how he stares at me. He must be hungry. Does Phuffy want a little snack?"

The cat squirmed.

"About those bloodstains on the window-sill," said the detective. "Would the cat attack anyone viciously enough to draw blood?"

"Certainly not!" said One. "He's just a harmless little house pet. We found him hiding under the bed scared stiff."

"Are you sure you can't remember any unusual incidents lately? Has anyone come to the house who might have seen the silver or jewelry? Anyone repair something recently? Window washer?"

"I wish I could be more helpful," said One, "but honestly, I can't think of a single suspect."

Phut Phat gave up!

Wriggling free, he jumped down from One's lap and walked to the door, stiff with disgust. He knew who it was. He *knew*! The man with the shiny stick! But it was useless to try to communicate with humans. The human mind was so tightly closed that nothing important would ever penetrate it.

The jiggle of keys caught Phut Phat's attention. He turned and saw Two swinging his key chain back and forth and saying nothing. Two always did more thinking than talking. Perhaps Phut Phat had been trying to communicate with the wrong mind.

Phut Phat froze and sat tall and began to concentrate. The key chain swung back and forth, and Phut Phat fastened his blue eyes on Two's forehead and concentrated and concentrated. The key chain swung back and forth, back and forth. Phut Phat kept concentrating.

"Wait a minute," said Two, coming out of his puzzled silence. "I just thought of something. Helen, remember that party we gave a couple of weeks ago? There was one guest we couldn't account for—a man with a silver cane."

"Why, yes! He was curious about the cage on the fire escape. Why didn't I think of him? Lieutenant, he was very interested in our silver collection."

Two said, "Does that suggest anything to you, Lieutenant?"

"Yes it does." The detective exchanged nods with his partner.

"This man," One volunteered, "had a very charming manner. He walked with a limp."

"We know him," the detective said grimly. "The limp is phony. We know his method and what you tell us fits perfectly. But we didn't know he was operating in this neighborhood again."

One said, "What I can't figure out is the blood on the windowsill."

Phut Phat arched his body in a long, long stretch and walked from the room. He was looking for a soft, dark, quiet place. Now he would sleep. He felt relaxed and satisfied. He had made vital contact with a human mind, so perhaps—after all—there was hope. Some day humans might learn the system, learn to open their minds and receive. They had a long way to go before then. But there was hope.

SELECTING DETAILS FROM THE STORY.
The following questions help you check your
reading comprehension. Put an *x* in the box
next to each correct answer.

1. The man with the silver cane asked One
   if he could
   - ☐ a. inspect Phut Phat's cage before
     leaving.
   - ☐ b. enter Phut Phat in a show.
   - ☐ c. interest her in purchasing some rare
     silver objects.

2. Phut Phat became alarmed when
   - ☐ a. a stranger called him a living
     sculpture.
   - ☐ b. One and Two went to see the
     Burmese kittens and left him alone.
   - ☐ c. he heard someone on the fire escape
     and something tapping at the
     window.

3. When One and Two returned from the
   Hendersons' house, they found Phut Phat
   - ☐ a. on top of a tall dresser.
   - ☐ b. hiding in a closet.
   - ☐ c. under the bed, brooding.

4. Nobody could figure out how the
   - ☐ a. burglar got into the house.
   - ☐ b. bloodstains got on the windowsill.
   - ☐ c. man with the cane knew where the
     silver was.

KNOWING NEW VOCABULARY WORDS. The
following questions check your vocabulary
skills. Put an *x* in the box next to each correct
answer.

1. Since One's mind kept hopping around,
   it was difficult for Phut Phat to convey
   his messages to her. As used here, the word
   convey means
   - ☐ a. send or communicate.
   - ☐ b. question or ask.
   - ☐ c. avoid or ignore.

2. Phut Phat went into the kitchen to
   investigate the aroma of shrimp and
   smoked oysters. What is the meaning of
   the word *aroma*?
   - ☐ a. price
   - ☐ b. odor
   - ☐ c. quantity

3. To Phut Phat, the man's presence seemed
   evil and sinister. Which of the following
   best defines the word *sinister*?
   - ☐ a. ordinary; usual
   - ☐ b. dull; boring
   - ☐ c. wicked; threatening

4. When he was no longer the center of
   attention, Phut Phat became annoyed
   and stalked out of the room with several
   irritable flicks of his tail. The word *irritable*
   means
   - ☐ a. angry.
   - ☐ b. attractive.
   - ☐ c. friendly.

☐ × 5 = ☐

NUMBER
CORRECT

YOUR
SCORE

☐ × 5 = ☐

NUMBER
CORRECT

YOUR
SCORE

IDENTIFYING STORY ELEMENTS. The following questions check your knowledge of story elements. Put an *x* in the box next to each correct answer.

1. "Phut Phat Concentrates" is *set* in a
   ☐ a. brownstone in a fashionable part of the city.
   ☐ b. country house in a charming village.
   ☐ c. fancy apartment in a busy town.

2. Identify the sentence that best *characterizes* Phut Phat.
   ☐ a. He was beautiful, intelligent, and somewhat vain.
   ☐ b. Because he was spoiled, he grew lazy and was no longer alert.
   ☐ c. He was neither curious nor courageous.

3. What happened first in the *plot* of the story?
   ☐ a. Phut Phat sprang at the man, ripping at him with his claws.
   ☐ b. Furniture was rearranged, and a stranger set up plates and glasses.
   ☐ c. A detective asked if there were any unusual incidents lately.

4. Which sentence best describes Phut Phat's *inner conflict*?
   ☐ a. He was annoyed that very few guests knew how to pay their respects to a cat.
   ☐ b. He was upset because One kept forgetting to give him liver on Sunday.
   ☐ c. He felt a very powerful urge to attack the stranger, but at the same time something within him said, "Stay!"

[   ] × 5 = [   ]
NUMBER   YOUR
CORRECT   SCORE

LOOKING AT CLOZE. The following questions use the cloze technique to check your reading comprehension. Complete the paragraph by filling in each blank with one of the words listed below. Each word appears in the story. Since there are five words and four blanks, one of the words will not be used.

One of the most beautiful and interesting breeds of cat is the _____ . It

is easy to _____ Siamese cats because of their striking blue eyes, their long, slender bodies, and the dark markings on their fur. Siamese cats seem to be more friendly and affectionate than other cats; they are _____ as "talkers." That is, they will meow loudly until they obtain the _____ they are seeking.

concentrate   attention

Siamese

identify   known

[   ] × 5 = [   ]
NUMBER   YOUR
CORRECT   SCORE

43

LEARNING HOW TO READ CRITICALLY.
The following questions check your critical
thinking skills. Put an *x* in the box next to
each correct answer.

1. We may infer that Two finally remembered
   the man with the silver cane because
   ☐ a. the police provided an excellent
        description of the suspect.
   ☐ b. Phut Phat eventually succeeded in
        communicating with Two.
   ☐ c. Two looked over a list of the guests
        who had been invited to the party.

2. When the burglar came upstairs, he was
   carrying a bulky load that he took to the
   window. The bulky load probably contained
   ☐ a. Phut Phat's cage.
   ☐ b. food that had been left over from
        the party.
   ☐ c. silver and other valuables.

3. Judging by what occurs in the story, we
   may conclude that the man with the silver
   cane was
   ☐ a. not invited to the party.
   ☐ b. invited to the party by either One
        or Two.
   ☐ c. invited to the party by one of the
        other guests.

4. Clues at the end of the story suggest that
   the burglar will
   ☐ a. break into the house again.
   ☐ b. eventually be caught by the police.
   ☐ c. never be seen or heard from again.

☐ × 5 = ☐

NUMBER   YOUR
CORRECT   SCORE

Improving Writing and Discussion Skills

- According to Phut Phat, cats are superior to human beings. What reasons
  might Phut Phat give to support his
  point of view? List at least five.
- When the detectives learned about
  the man with the silver cane, they
  recognized his method at once.
  What was the man's "method"? Use
  examples from the story when you
  answer the question.
- One thing that is unusual about
  "Phut Phat Concentrates" is that the
  events are seen through the eyes of
  a cat. Suppose that you are Phut Phat.
  Describe your encounter with the
  man who broke into the house. Make
  your account of the incident as vivid
  as possible.

Use the boxes below to total your scores
for the exercises. Then write your score on
pages 140 and 141.

☐ SELECTING DETAILS FROM THE STORY
+
☐ KNOWING NEW VOCABULARY WORDS
+
☐ IDENTIFYING STORY ELEMENTS
+
☐ LOOKING AT CLOZE
+
☐ LEARNING HOW TO READ CRITICALLY
▼
☐ Score Total: Story 4

5. A Day's Wait

by Ernest Hemingway

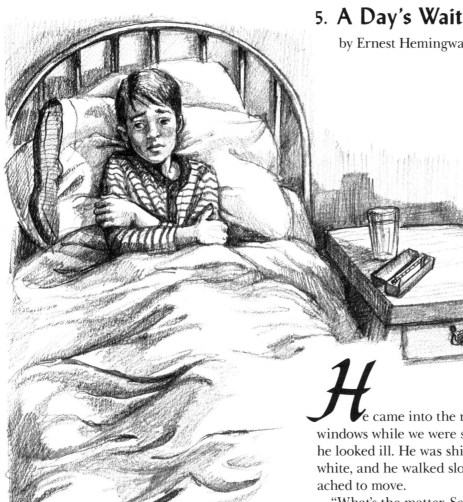

Meet the Author

Ernest Hemingway (1899–1961) is considered
one of the major figures in modern American
literature. His lean, powerful style of writing
has influenced many other authors. Born in
Oak Park, Illinois, Hemingway began his career
as a journalist and later traveled and lived around
the world. In 1953 his novel, *The Old Man and
the Sea,* won a Pulitzer Prize. The following
year, Hemingway received the Nobel Prize
for literature. "A Day's Wait" is based on an
incident involving the illness of one of his sons.

*H*e came into the room to shut the
windows while we were still in bed and I saw
he looked ill. He was shivering, his face was
white, and he walked slowly as though it
ached to move.

"What's the matter, Schatz?"

"I've got a headache."

"You'd better go back to bed."

"No. I'm all right."

"You go to bed. I'll see you when I'm
dressed."

But when I came downstairs he was
dressed, sitting by the fire, looking a very
sick and miserable boy of nine years. When
I put my hand on his forehead I knew he
had a fever.

"You go up to bed," I said, "you're sick."

"I'm all right," he said.

When the doctor came he took the boy's
temperature.

"What is it?" I asked him.

"One hundred and two."

Downstairs, the doctor left three different medicines in different-colored capsules with instructions for giving them. One was to bring down the fever, another a purgative,[1] the third to overcome an acid condition. The germs of influenza can only exist in an acid condition, he explained. He seemed to know all about influenza and said there was nothing to worry about if the fever did not go above one hundred and four degrees. This was a light epidemic of flu and there was no danger if you avoided pneumonia.

Back in the room I wrote the boy's temperature down and made a note of the time to give the various capsules.

"Do you want me to read to you?"

"All right. If you want to," said the boy. His face was very white and there were dark areas under his eyes. He lay still in the bed and seemed very detached from what was going on.

I read aloud from Howard Pyle's *Book of Pirates*; but I could see he was not following what I was reading.

"Just the same, so far," he said.

I sat at the foot of the bed and read to myself while I waited for it to be time to give another capsule. It would have been natural for him to go to sleep, but when I looked up he was looking at the foot of the bed, looking very strangely.

"Why don't you try to go to sleep? I'll wake you up for the medicine."

"I'd rather stay awake."

After a while he said to me, "You don't have to stay in here with me, Papa, if it bothers you."

"It doesn't bother me."

"No, I mean you don't have to stay if it's going to bother you."

I thought perhaps he was a little light-headed and after giving him the prescribed capsules at 11:00 I went out for a while.

It was a bright, cold day, the ground covered with a sleet that had frozen so that it seemed as if all the bare trees, the bushes, the cut brush, and all the grass and the bare ground had been varnished with ice. I took the young Irish setter for a little walk up the road and along a frozen creek, but it was difficult to stand or walk on the glassy surface and the red dog slipped and slithered and I fell twice. . . .

At the house they said the boy had refused to let anyone come into the room.

"You can't come in," he said. "You mustn't get what I have."

I went up to him and found him in exactly the position I had left him, white-faced, but with the tops of his cheeks flushed by the fever, staring still, as he had stared, at the foot of the bed.

I took his temperature.

"What is it?"

"Something like a hundred," I said. It was one hundred and two and four tenths.

"It was a hundred and two," he said.

"Who said so?"

"The doctor."

"Your temperature is all right," I said. "It's nothing to worry about."

"I don't worry," he said, "but I can't keep from thinking."

"Don't think," I said. "Just take it easy."

"I'm taking it easy," he said and looked straight ahead. He was evidently holding tight onto himself about something.

---

1. **purgative:** a medicine to clean out the system.

"Take this with water."

"Do you think it will do any good?"

"Of course it will."

I sat down and opened the *Pirate* book and commenced to read, but I could see he was not following, so I stopped.

"About what time do you think I'm going to die?" he asked.

"What?"

"About how long will it be before I die?"

"You aren't going to die. What's the matter with you?"

"Oh, yes I am. I heard him say a hundred and two."

"People don't die with a fever of one hundred and two. That's a silly way to talk."

"I know they do. At school in France the boys told me you can't live with forty-four degrees. I've got a hundred and two."

He had been waiting to die all day, ever since 9:00 in the morning.

"You poor Schatz," I said. "Poor old Schatz. It's like miles and kilometers. You aren't going to die. That's a different thermometer. On that thermometer thirty-seven is normal. On this kind it's ninety-eight."

"Are you sure?"

"Absolutely," I said. "It's like miles and kilometers. You know, like how many kilometers we make when we do seventy miles in the car."

"Oh," he said.

But his gaze at the foot of the bed relaxed slowly. The hold over himself relaxed, too, finally, and the next day it was very slack and he cried very easily at little things that were of no importance.

SELECTING DETAILS FROM THE STORY.
The following questions help you check your reading comprehension. Put an *x* in the box next to each correct answer.

1. Schatz was ill with
   - ☐ a. a bad cold.
   - ☐ b. pneumonia.
   - ☐ c. the flu.

2. The doctor said that Schatz had a temperature of
   - ☐ a. ninety-eight.
   - ☐ b. one hundred and two.
   - ☐ c. a little over one hundred and four.

3. The boy refused to let anyone come into the room because he
   - ☐ a. was too exhausted to speak to anyone.
   - ☐ b. was in a bad mood and didn't want company.
   - ☐ c. didn't want anyone to catch what he had.

4. Schatz had been waiting all day to
   - ☐ a. die.
   - ☐ b. feel a little better.
   - ☐ c. recover completely.

KNOWING NEW VOCABULARY WORDS.
The following questions check your vocabulary skills. Put an *x* in the box next to each correct answer.

1. Papa gave his son the medicine that the doctor had prescribed. What is the meaning of the word *prescribed*?
   - ☐ a. tasted
   - ☐ b. discovered
   - ☐ c. ordered

2. The boy was pale, but the tops of his cheeks were flushed by the fever. As used here, the word *flushed* means
   - ☐ a. made red.
   - ☐ b. washed away.
   - ☐ c. torn apart.

3. It was difficult to stand or walk on the glassy, icy surface, so the dog slipped and slithered. Define the word *slithered*.
   - ☐ a. slid
   - ☐ b. trotted
   - ☐ c. barked

4. Tired and ill, the boy lay quite still in the bed, detached from everything that was going on. As used in this sentence, the word *detached* means
   - ☐ a. involved with.
   - ☐ b. pleased about.
   - ☐ c. not interested in.

☐ × 5 = ☐

NUMBER CORRECT   YOUR SCORE

☐ × 5 = ☐

NUMBER CORRECT   YOUR SCORE

IDENTIFYING STORY ELEMENTS. The following questions check your knowledge of story elements. Put an x in the box next to each correct answer.

1. Where is "A Day's Wait" *set*?
   ☐ a. in a hospital
   ☐ b. in a doctor's office
   ☐ c. in a bedroom

2. What happened last in the *plot* of the story?
   ☐ a. The doctor left three different medicines with instructions for giving them.
   ☐ b. Papa took the dog for a walk up the road and along the creek.
   ☐ c. The boy cried easily at things that were of no importance.

3. "On that thermometer thirty-seven is normal." This line of *dialogue* was spoken by
   ☐ a. Schatz.
   ☐ b. Papa.
   ☐ c. the doctor.

4. What is the *mood* of "A Day's Wait"?
   ☐ a. serious
   ☐ b. humorous
   ☐ c. mysterious

LOOKING AT CLOZE. The following questions use the cloze technique to check your reading comprehension. Complete the paragraph by filling in each blank with one of the words listed below. Each word appears in the story. Since there are five words and four blanks, one of the words will not be used.

Each year thousands of people become

_____ with the flu. The
        1

symptoms are similar to those of a cold,

except that the victim usually feels very weak

and often has a _____ . Among
                          2

the various _____ are headache,
                    3

chills, and aches and pains. The flu, or

_____ , generally lasts from a
        4

couple of days to several weeks.

influenza   ill

complaints

fever   capsules

NUMBER CORRECT ☐ × 5 = ☐ YOUR SCORE

NUMBER CORRECT ☐ × 5 = ☐ YOUR SCORE

LEARNING HOW TO READ CRITICALLY.
The following questions check your critical
thinking skills. Put an *x* in the box next to
each correct answer.

1. Schatz believed he was going to die
   because he thought that
   □ a. the doctor had given him the wrong
         medicines.
   □ b. no one knew how to treat his rare
         disease.
   □ c. his fever was too high for him to
         survive.

2. Schatz probably did not follow the story
   his father was reading because
   □ a. the story was too difficult for the
         boy to understand.
   □ b. Papa was reading very softly.
   □ c. the boy couldn't concentrate since
         he was thinking about his own
         death.

3. It is fair to say that Schatz faced death
   with
   □ a. courage.
   □ b. anger.
   □ c. hope.

4. The last paragraph of the story suggests
   that the incident
   □ a. had little or no effect on Schatz.
   □ b. affected Schatz greatly.
   □ c. seemed amusing to Schatz.

	× 5 =	
NUMBER CORRECT		YOUR SCORE

Improving Writing and Discussion Skills

- Why is "A Day's Wait" an appropriate
  title for the story? Make up another
  name for the selection, one with the
  word "Encounter" in the title.
- In what ways did Schatz act strangely?
  Do you think the father should have
  said something to Schatz when he
  acted that way? Why?
- Why did Schatz wait so long to
  mention what was on his mind? Show
  that the boy had been controlling
  his emotions, and that he finally
  "let go."

Use the boxes below to total your scores
for the exercises. Then write your score on
pages 140 and 141.

	SELECTING DETAILS FROM THE STORY
+	
	KNOWING NEW VOCABULARY WORDS
+	
	IDENTIFYING STORY ELEMENTS
+	
	LOOKING AT CLOZE
+	
	LEARNING HOW TO READ CRITICALLY
▼	
	Score Total: Story 5

6. All the Years of Her Life

by Morley Callaghan

hey were closing the drugstore, and Alfred Higgins, who had just taken off his white jacket, was putting on his coat and getting ready to go home. The little grey-haired man, Sam Carr, who owned the drugstore, was bending down behind the cash register, and when Alfred Higgins passed him he looked up and said softly, "Just a moment, Alfred. One moment before you go."

The soft, confident, quiet way in which Sam Carr spoke made Alfred start to button his coat nervously. He felt sure his face was white. Sam Carr usually said "Good night" brusquely, without looking up. In the six months he had been working in the drugstore Alfred had never heard his employer speak softly like that. His heart began to beat so loud it was hard for him to get his breath. "What is it, Mr. Carr?" he asked.

Meet the Author

Morley Callaghan (1903–1990) is one of Canada's best-known novelists and short-story writers. Born in Toronto, where he lived and worked most of his life, Callaghan gave up a career in law to concentrate on writing. Encouraged by Ernest Hemingway, whom he met on a trip to Paris, Callaghan gained recognition when his first novel, *Strange Fugitive,* was published. His most popular work is *Now that April's Here,* a collection of short stories.

"Maybe you'd be good enough to take a few things out of your pocket and leave them here before you go," Sam Carr said.

"What things? What are you talking about?"

"You've got a compact and a lipstick and at least two tubes of toothpaste in your pockets, Alfred."

"What do you mean? Do you think I'm crazy?" Alfred blustered. His face got red and he knew he looked fierce with indignation. But Sam Carr, standing by the door with his blue eyes shining bright behind his glasses and his lips moving underneath his grey mustache, only nodded his head a few times, and then Alfred grew very frightened and he didn't know what to say. Slowly he raised his hand and dipped it into his pocket, and with his eyes never meeting Sam Carr's eyes, he took out a blue compact and two tubes of toothpaste and a lipstick, and he placed them one by one on the counter.

"Petty thieving, eh, Alfred?" Sam Carr said. "And maybe you'd be good enough to tell me how long this has been going on."

"This is the first time I ever took anything."

"So now you think you'll tell me a lie, eh? What kind of a sap do I look like, huh? I don't know what goes on in my own store, eh? I tell you you've been doing this pretty steady," Sam Carr said as he went over and stood behind the cash register.

Ever since Alfred had left school he had been getting into trouble wherever he worked. He lived at home with his mother and father, who was a printer. His two older brothers were married and his sister had got married last year, and it would have been all right for his parents now if Alfred had only been able to keep a job.

While Sam Carr smiled and stroked the side of his face very delicately with the tips of his fingers, Alfred began to feel that familiar terror growing in him that had been in him every time he had got into such trouble.

"I liked you," Sam Carr was saying. "I liked you and would have trusted you, and now look what I got to do." While Alfred watched with his alert, frightened blue eyes, Sam Carr drummed with his fingers on the counter. "I don't like to call a cop in point-blank," he was saying as he looked very worried. "You're a fool, and maybe I should call your father and tell him you're a fool. Maybe I should let them know I'm going to have you locked up."

"My father's not at home. He's a printer. He works nights," Alfred said.

"Who's at home?"

"My mother, I guess."

"Then we'll see what she says." Sam Carr went to the phone and dialed the number. Alfred was not so much ashamed, but there was that deep fright growing in him, and he blurted out arrogantly, "Just a minute. You don't need to draw anybody else in. You don't need to tell her." He wanted to sound like a swaggering, big guy who could look after himself, yet the old, childish hope was in him, the longing that someone at home would come and help him. "Yeah, that's right, he's in trouble," Mr. Carr was saying. "Yeah, your boy works for me. You'd better come down in a hurry." When he was finished Mr. Carr went over to the door and looked out at the street and watched the people passing in the late summer night. "I'll keep my eye out for a cop," was all he said.

Alfred knew how his mother would come rushing in; she would rush in with her eyes blazing, or maybe she would be crying, and she would push him away, when he tried to talk to her, and make him feel her dreadful contempt; yet he longed that she might come before Mr. Carr saw the cop on the beat passing the door.

While they waited—and it seemed a long time—they did not speak, and when at last they heard someone tapping on the closed door, Mr. Carr, turning the latch, said crisply, "Come in, Mrs. Higgins." He looked hard-faced and stern.

Mrs. Higgins must have been going to bed when he telephoned, for her hair was tucked in loosely under her hat. She came in, large and plump, with a little smile on her friendly face. Most of the store lights had been turned out and at first she did not see Alfred, who was standing in the shadow at the end of the counter. Yet as soon as she saw him she did not look as Alfred thought she would look; she smiled, her blue eyes never wavered, and with calmness and dignity, she put out her hand to Mr. Carr and said politely, "I'm Mrs. Higgins. I'm Alfred's mother."

Mr. Carr was a bit embarrassed by her lack of terror and her simplicity, and he hardly knew what to say to her, so she asked, "Is Alfred in trouble?"

"He is. He's been taking things from the store. I caught him red-handed. Little things like compacts and toothpaste and lipsticks. Stuff he can sell easily," the proprietor said.

As she listened Mrs. Higgins looked at Alfred sometimes and nodded her head sadly, and when Sam Carr had finished she said gravely, "Is it so, Alfred?"

"Yes."

"Why have you been doing it?"

"I been spending money, I guess."

"On what?"

"Going around with the guys, I guess," Alfred said.

Mrs. Higgins put out her hand and touched Sam Carr's arm with understanding gentleness, and speaking as though afraid of disturbing him, she said, "If you would only listen to me before doing anything." Her simple earnestness made her shy; her humility made her falter and look away, but in a moment she was smiling gravely again, and she said with a kind of patient dignity, "What did you intend to do, Mr. Carr?"

"I was going to get a cop. That's what I ought to do."

"Yes, I suppose so. It's not for me to say, because he's my son. Yet I sometimes think a little good advice is the best thing for a boy when he's at a certain period in his life."

Alfred couldn't understand his mother's quiet composure, for if they had been at home and someone had suggested that he was going to be arrested, he knew she would be in a rage and would cry out against him. Yet now she was standing there with that gentle, pleading smile, saying, "I wonder if you don't think it would be better just to let him come home with me. He looks like a big fellow, doesn't he? It takes some of them a long time to get any sense," and they both stared at Alfred, who shifted away with a bit of light shining for a moment on his thin face.

But even while he was turning away uneasily, Alfred was realizing that Mr. Carr had become aware that his mother was really a fine woman; he knew that Sam Carr was puzzled by his mother, as if he had expected her to come in and plead with him tearfully, and instead he was being made to feel a bit ashamed by her vast tolerance. While there was only the sound of the mother's soft, assured voice in the store, Mr. Carr began to nod his head encouragingly at her.

Without being alarmed, while being just large and still and simple and hopeful, she was becoming dominant there in the dimly lit store. "Of course, I don't want to be harsh," Mr. Carr was saying. "I'll tell you what I'll do. I'll just fire him and let it go at that. How's that?" and he got up and shook hands with Mrs. Higgins, bowing low to her in deep respect.

There was such warmth and gratitude in the way she said, "I'll never forget your kindness," that Mr. Carr began to feel warm and genial himself.

"Sorry we had to meet this way," he said. "But, I'm glad I got in touch with you. Just wanted to do the right thing, that's all," he said.

"It's better to meet like this than never, isn't it?" she said. Suddenly they clasped hands as if they liked each other, as if they had known each other a long time. "Good night, sir," she said.

"Good night, Mrs. Higgins. I'm truly sorry," he said.

The mother and son walked along the street together, and the mother was taking a long, firm stride as she looked ahead with her stern face full of worry. Alfred was afraid to speak to her; he was afraid of the silence that was between them too, so he only looked ahead, for the excitement and relief were still pretty strong in him; but in a little while, going along like that in silence made him terribly aware of the strength and the sternness in her; he began to wonder what she was thinking of as she stared ahead so grimly; she seemed to have forgotten that he walked beside her; so when they were passing under the railway bridge and the rumble of the train seemed to break the silence, he said in his old, blustering way, "I certainly won't get in a jam like that again."

"Be quiet. Don't speak to me. You've disgraced me again and again," she said bitterly.

"That's the last time. That's all I'm saying."

"Have the decency to be quiet," she snapped.

When they were at home she made him feel afraid again when she said, without even looking at him, "You're a bad lot. It's one thing after another and always has been. Why do you stand there stupidly? Go to bed, why don't you?" When he was going, she said, "I'm going to make myself a cup of tea. Mind, now, not a word about tonight to your father."

While Alfred was undressing in his bedroom, he heard his mother moving around the kitchen. She filled the kettle and put it on the stove. She moved a chair. As he listened there was no shame in him, just wonder and a kind of admiration of her strength and repose. He could still see Sam Carr nodding his head encouragingly to her; he could hear her talking simply and earnestly, and as he sat on his bed he felt a pride in her strength. "She certainly was smooth," he thought. "Gee, I'd like to tell her she sounded swell."

At last he got up and went along to the kitchen, and when he was at the door he saw his mother pouring herself a cup of tea. He watched and he didn't move. Her face, as she sat there, was a frightened, broken face utterly unlike the face of a woman who had been so assured a little while ago in the drugstore. When she reached out and lifted the kettle to pour hot water in her cup, her hand trembled and the water splashed on the stove. Leaning back in the chair, she sighed and lifted the cup to her lips, and her lips were groping loosely as if they would never reach the cup. She swallowed the hot tea eagerly, and then she straightened up in relief, though her hand holding the cup still trembled. She looked very old.

It seemed to Alfred that this was the way it had been every time he had been in trouble before, that this trembling had really been in her as she hurried out to the drugstore. Now he felt all that his mother had been thinking of as they walked along the street together a little while ago. He watched his mother, and he never spoke, but at that moment his youth seemed to be over; he knew all the years of her life by the way her hand trembled as she raised the cup to her lips. It seemed to him that this was the first time he had ever looked upon his mother.

SELECTING DETAILS FROM THE STORY.
The following questions help you check your
reading comprehension. Put an *x* in the box
next to each correct answer.

1. Sam Carr accused Alfred Higgins of
   - ☐ a. taking money out of the cash register.
   - ☐ b. stealing small articles.
   - ☐ c. arriving late to work.

2. After speaking to Mrs. Higgins, Mr. Carr
   decided to
   - ☐ a. turn Alfred over to the police.
   - ☐ b. give Alfred another chance in the
     store.
   - ☐ c. fire Alfred and let it go at that.

3. On the way home from the store,
   Mrs. Higgins told Alfred
   - ☐ a. not to speak to her.
   - ☐ b. to look for another job.
   - ☐ c. to tell his father what happened.

4. At the end of the story, it seemed to
   Alfred that
   - ☐ a. his mother suddenly was happy.
   - ☐ b. his mother looked younger than she
     actually was.
   - ☐ c. he had never really looked at his
     mother before.

KNOWING NEW VOCABULARY WORDS. The
following questions check your vocabulary
skills. Put an *x* in the box next to each correct
answer.

1. "Just a minute," Alfred blurted out, trying
   to sound like a swaggering guy who could
   look after himself. As used here, the word
   swaggering means
   - ☐ a. bold or confident.
   - ☐ b. young or youthful.
   - ☐ c. fearful or cowardly.

2. Sam Carr usually spoke brusquely, but this
   time his voice was soft and quiet. The
   word *brusquely* means
   - ☐ a. harshly.
   - ☐ b. foolishly.
   - ☐ c. nervously.

3. Alfred's mother showed such warmth and
   gratitude that Mr. Carr began to feel
   genial himself. Which of the following
   best defines the word *genial*?
   - ☐ a. jealous; envious
   - ☐ b. kindly; friendly
   - ☐ c. furious; angry

4. When Alfred got into trouble, his mother's
   eyes would blaze and she would push him
   away with dreadful contempt. When you
   feel *contempt* for someone, you
   - ☐ a. admire or respect that person.
   - ☐ b. ask that person for advice.
   - ☐ c. consider that person low or
     worthless.

NUMBER CORRECT	× 5 =	YOUR SCORE

NUMBER CORRECT	× 5 =	YOUR SCORE

IDENTIFYING STORY ELEMENTS. The following questions check your knowledge of story elements. Put an *x* in the box next to each correct answer.

1. What happened first in the *plot* of "All the Years of Her Life"?
   - [ ] a. Mrs. Higgins introduced herself to Mr. Carr.
   - [ ] b. Mr. Carr asked Albert to take a few things out of his pocket.
   - [ ] c. Alfred watched his mother drink a cup of tea.

2. In the story there is *conflict* between
   - [ ] a. Mr. Carr and Mrs. Higgins.
   - [ ] b. Mr. and Mrs. Higgins.
   - [ ] c. Alfred and his mother.

3. What was Alfred's *motive* for taking the items?
   - [ ] a. He wanted to give them away as presents.
   - [ ] b. He planned to sell them for spending money.
   - [ ] c. He wanted to get even with Mr. Carr for criticizing him.

4. Which statement best expresses the *theme* of the story?
   - [ ] a. A dramatic incident leads a young man to recognize his mother's concern about him.
   - [ ] b. A mother punishes her son for bringing shame to the family.
   - [ ] c. If you steal things, the chances are that you will be caught.

	× 5 =	
NUMBER CORRECT		YOUR SCORE

LOOKING AT CLOZE. The following questions use the cloze technique to check your reading comprehension. Complete the paragraph by filling in each blank with one of the words listed below. Each word appears in the story. Since there are five words and four blanks, one of the words will not be used.

Next to coffee, _____ is the
1

most popular drink in the world. In England,

having afternoon tea around four o'clock

is a custom _____ enjoyed by
2

millions of people. In China and Japan, tea

plays a part in _____ religious
3

and social ceremonies. It goes without

_____ that in the United States,
4

iced tea is an especially popular warm-

weather drink.

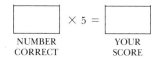

certain   tea

assured

usually   saying

	× 5 =	
NUMBER CORRECT		YOUR SCORE

LEARNING HOW TO READ CRITICALLY.
The following questions check your critical
thinking skills. Put an x in the box next to
each correct answer.

1. At the end of the story Alfred realized
   that
   ☐ a. his mother was very proud of him.
   ☐ b. he could have handled the situation
        without his mother's help.
   ☐ c. his mother seemed calm and strong
        in the store, but she was actually
        frightened and upset.

2. Evidence in the story indicates that
   ☐ a. Alfred had never gotten into trouble
        before.
   ☐ b. Mrs. Higgins was very worried about
        her son.
   ☐ c. Mr. Carr was unfeeling and stubborn.

3. How did Mrs. Higgins persuade Mr. Carr
   to let Alfred go home with her?
   ☐ a. by gently convincing him that it was
        the right thing to do
   ☐ b. by challenging his authority and
        threatening him
   ☐ c. by offering to pay him for any losses
        he had suffered

4. The last paragraph of the story suggests
   that Alfred
   ☐ a. will continue to disgrace his mother.
   ☐ b. felt bitter toward his mother for the
        way she acted.
   ☐ c. matured greatly as a result of the
        day's experience.

	× 5 =	
NUMBER CORRECT		YOUR SCORE

Improving Writing and Discussion Skills

- As he watched his mother drinking
  tea in the kitchen, Alfred felt at that
  moment that "his youth seemed to
  be over; he knew all the years of her
  life by the way her hand trembled
  as she raised the cup to her lips."
  What is the meaning of the words
  quoted here?
- Did Mr. Carr do the right thing in
  simply firing Alfred? Explain. Do
  you think it likely that Alfred will
  steal again? Why? If you had been
  Mr. Carr, what would you have done?
- Suppose that Alfred decided to write
  a letter to Mr. Carr. What do you
  think the letter would say?

Use the boxes below to total your scores
for the exercises. Then write your score on
pages 140 and 141.

☐ + SELECTING DETAILS FROM THE STORY

☐ + KNOWING NEW VOCABULARY WORDS

☐ + IDENTIFYING STORY ELEMENTS

☐ + LOOKING AT CLOZE

☐ ▼ LEARNING HOW TO READ CRITICALLY

☐ Score Total: Story 6

7. The Love Letter

by Jack Finney

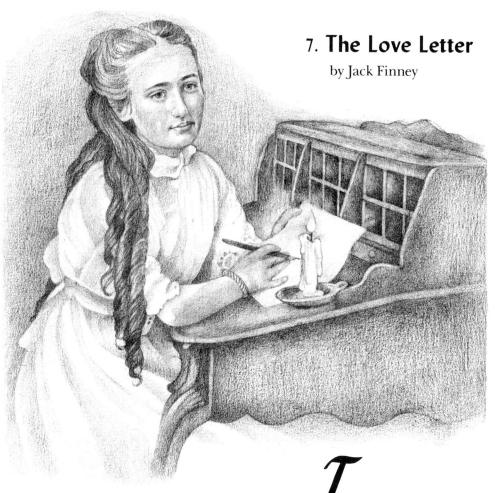

I've heard of secret drawers in old desks, of course—who hasn't? But the day I bought my desk I wasn't thinking of secret drawers, and I didn't think there was any mystery about it. I spotted it in a secondhand store near my apartment, went in to look it over, and the proprietor told me where he got it.

It came from one of the last of those big old houses built in the middle of the nineteenth century, in Brooklyn. They were tearing it down over on Brock Place, a few blocks away, and he'd bought the desk along with some other furniture and things.

It didn't stir my imagination particularly. I never wondered or cared who might have

Meet the Author

Jack Finney (1911–   ) is one of today's most popular writers of science fiction and fantasy. Of his numerous short stories and novels, six of them have been made into motion pictures. The most famous of these is *The Invasion of the Body Snatchers*, a science-fiction classic. Born in Milwaukee, Wisconsin, Finney currently lives near San Francisco, California.

used it long ago. I bought it and lugged it home because it was cheap and because it was small—a little wall desk without legs that I fastened to my living room wall with heavy screws.

I'm twenty-four years old, tall and thin, and I live in Brooklyn and work in Manhattan. When you're twenty-four and a bachelor, you usually figure you'll be married before too much longer, and since they tell me that takes money, I bring work home from the office once in a while. And maybe every couple of weeks or so I write a letter to my folks in Florida. So I'd been needing a desk. I'd been trying to work at a wobbly little end table that I couldn't get my legs under.

I bought the desk one Saturday afternoon and spent an hour or so fastening it to the wall. Then I stood back and admired it for a while. It was made of heavy wood, with a slanted top like a kid's school desk, and with a space underneath to put things into. The back of it rose at least two feet above the desk top and was full of pigeonholes—you know, little compartments. Underneath the pigeonholes was a row of three little drawers. I pulled a chair up and sat down at the desk to try it for height. Then I took a shower and got dressed and went into Manhattan because I had a date there that night.

I'm trying to be honest about what happened, and I'm convinced that includes the way I felt when I got home that night. I'd had a good enough time that evening. We'd gone to an early movie that wasn't too bad, then had dinner afterward. And my date, Roberta Haig, is pretty nice—bright, pleasant, good-looking. But walking home from the subway in the Brooklyn streets,

which were quiet and deserted, it occurred to me that while I'd probably see her again, I didn't really care whether I did or not. And I wondered, as I often did lately, whether I'd ever meet a woman I desperately wanted to be with—the only way I'd ever get married, it seemed to me.

When I stepped into the apartment I knew I wasn't going to feel like sleep for a while. I was restless, and I took off my coat and yanked down my tie, wondering whether I wanted some coffee. Then—I'd half forgotten about it—I saw the desk I'd bought that afternoon, and I walked over and sat down at it.

I reached into one of the pigeonholes, and my hand and sleeve came out streaked with dust. I pulled open one of the three little drawers and there was a scrap of paper there, nothing else. I pulled the drawer all the way out and held it up in my hand, admiring its construction. And then it suddenly occurred to me that the little drawer in my hand was only six inches deep, while the top of the desk extended at least a foot back.

I shoved my hand into the opening and could feel, with my fingertips, the handle of a secret drawer hidden in back of the drawer I'd removed.

I pulled out the secret drawer, and for an instant, grew excited when I glimpsed some papers inside it. Then I felt a stab of disappointment when I saw what they were. There was some plain white writing paper, yellowed with age at the edges, the sheets all blank. There were three or four blank envelopes and underneath them a small, round glass bottle of ink. Because it had been upside down, the cork fit tightly in the mouth of the bottle, and about a third of the ink still remained. Next to the bottle was a plain, black wooden pen, its point reddish-black with old ink. There was nothing else in the drawer.

And then, as I was putting the things back into the drawer, I felt that one of the envelopes was slightly thicker than the others and that it was sealed. I ripped it open to find the letter inside. The folded paper opened stiffly with age, and even before I saw the date, I knew this letter was *old*. The handwriting was beautifully clear, the letters elegant and perfectly formed, the capitals, especially, a whirl of dainty curls. The ink was rust-black, the date at the top of the page was May 14, 1882, and reading it, I saw that it was a love letter. It began:

Dearest!

Pappa, Mamma, and Willy have long since retired to sleep. Now, the night far advanced, the house silent, I alone remain awake, at last free to speak to you as I choose. Yes, I am willing to say it! Heart of mine I crave your bold glance, I long for the tender warmth of your look! I welcome and prize your ardent gaze. For how else should I take these but as honor to me?

I smiled a little. It was hard to believe that people once expressed themselves using elaborate phrases like these. But they had. The letter continued, and I wondered why it had never been sent.

Dear one: Do not ever change your ways. Never address me other than in the way my actions should deserve. If I act foolishly, scoff at me sweetly if you will. But if I speak earnestly, respond seriously with all the care you deem worthy of my thoughts. For, oh my

beloved, I am sick to death of the superior smile which greets a woman's true feelings. I am angered and repelled by one who is not sincere, one who offers a false show of interest in all I hold dear. I am speaking of the man I am to marry! If you could but save me from that!

But you cannot. You are everything I prize: warmly and honestly loving, respectful in heart as well as in manner, true and caring. You are as I wish you to be—for you exist only in my mind. But though you live only in my imagination, and though I shall never see your like, you are more dear to me than the man to whom I am engaged.

I think of you constantly. I dream of you. I speak with you—in my mind and heart. If only you existed outside them! Sweetheart, good night. Dream of me, too.

With all my love, I am,
your Helen

At the bottom of the page, as I'm sure she'd been taught in school, was written, "Miss Helen Elizabeth Worley, Brooklyn, New York." And as I stared down at it now I was no longer smiling at this cry from the heart in the middle of a long-ago night.

The night is a strange time when you're alone in it, the rest of your world asleep. If I'd found that letter in the daytime, I'd have smiled and shown it to a few friends, then forgotten it. But alone here now, a window partly open, a cool late-at-night breeze stirring the quiet air, it was impossible to think of the woman who had written this letter as a very old woman, or one long since dead. As I read her words, she seemed alive and real to me, sitting—or so I pictured her—pen in hand at this desk, in a long, white, old-fashioned dress, in the dead of night like this, here in Brooklyn not far away from where I now sat. And my heart went out to her as I stared down at her secret, hopeless appeal against the world and time she lived in.

I am trying to explain why I answered that letter. There in the silence of that spring night, it seemed natural enough to remove the cork from the old bottle of ink, pick up the pen beside it, and then, spreading a sheet of yellowing old notepaper on the desk, to begin to write. I felt that I was communicating with a still-living young woman when I wrote:

Helen:

I have just read the letter in the secret drawer of your desk, and I wish I knew how I could possibly help you. I can't tell what you might think of me if there were a way I could reach you. But you are someone I am certain I would like to know. I hope you are beautiful, but you needn't be. You're a woman I could like, and maybe ardently. And if I did, I promise you I'd be true and loving. Do the best you can, Helen Elizabeth Worley, in the time and place you are. I can't reach you or help you. But I'll think of you. And maybe I'll dream of you, too.

Yours,
Jake Belknap

Maybe what I did seems foolish. Still, I folded the paper, put it into one of the old envelopes, and sealed it. Then I dipped the pen into the old ink, and wrote "Miss Helen Worley" on the face of the envelope.

It's hard to explain. You'd have to have been where I was and felt as I did to understand it, but I wanted to mail that letter. I was suddenly determined to complete what I'd begun.

On my hall closet shelf, in a box I hadn't looked at in years, I found my old stamp album. I turned the pages of that beat-up old album to the stamps I remembered buying from another kid. There they were, lightly fastened to the page with a little gummed paper hinge: two, two-cent United States stamps, issued in 1869. For all I knew, they might have been worth a fair amount of money by now. But back at the desk, I pulled off one of the stamps, licked the back of it, and fastened it to the faintly yellowing old envelope. Then, almost in a trance, I picked up the letter and walked out of my apartment.

Brock Place, three blocks away, was deserted when I reached it. Then, as I walked on, my letter in my hand, there stood the old house. It was in the center of a wide, weed-grown lot, black-etched in the moonlight. The old roof was gone, the interior nearly gutted, the yard strewn with boards and chunks of torn plaster.

I walked through the opening where a gate had once hung, up the cracked pavement toward the wide old porch. And there, on one of the posts, I saw the house number carved deeply into the old wood. I took out my ink and pen and copied the number carefully onto my envelope. I printed "972" under the name of the woman who had once lived here—Helen Worley—"Brock Place, Brooklyn, New York." Then I turned toward the street again, my envelope in my hand.

There was a mailbox at the next corner,

and I stopped next to it. I stood there for a moment and then walked on past the box. I crossed the street and turned right, suddenly knowing exactly where I was going.

I walked four blocks through the night, turned left, and walked half a block more. Then I turned onto the worn stone steps of the Wister Post Office.

It must easily be one of the oldest post offices in our borough, built, I suppose, not much after the Civil War. I can't imagine that the inside has changed much at all. The floor is marble, the ceiling high, the woodwork dark and carved. The outer lobby is open at all times, and as I pushed through the old swinging doors, I saw that it was deserted. The lobby itself was silent and dim, and as I walked across the stone floor, I knew I was doing what Brooklynites had done for many generations.

I pushed the worn brass plate open and dropped the letter into the silent blackness of the slot. It disappeared forever with no sound. Then I turned and left to walk home, feeling I'd done everything I possibly could in response to the cry for help I'd found in the secret drawer of the old desk I'd bought.

Next morning I felt the way almost anyone might. Remembering what I'd done the night before, I grinned, feeling foolish. But at the same time, I was secretly pleased with myself. I was glad that I had written and mailed that letter. And now I realized why I hadn't put any return address on the envelope. I didn't want it to come back to me with the words NO SUCH PERSON—or whatever the phrase is—stamped on the envelope. There'd once

been this young woman, and last night she still existed for me. And I didn't want to see my letter to her returned, rubber-stamped and unopened, to prove that there no longer was.

I was extremely busy all the next week. More often than not I had lunch at my desk in the office and worked several evenings, in addition.

That Friday evening I worked at home, sitting at my desk. But once more now, Helen Elizabeth Worley was in my mind. I worked steadily all evening, and it was around twelve-thirty when I finished. I opened the little center drawer of the desk into which I'd put some rubber bands and paper clips. I took out a clip, fastened some pages together, and sat back in my chair. The little center drawer was half open as I'd left it, and then, as my eye fell on it, I realized suddenly that *it*, too, of course, must have a secret drawer behind it.

I hadn't thought of that. It simply hadn't occurred to me the week before, in my interest and excitement over the letter I'd found behind the first drawer of the row. And I'd been too busy all week to think of it since. But now I pulled the center drawer all the way out, reached behind it, and touched the little handle there. Then I pulled out the second secret little drawer.

I'll tell you what I think, what I'm certain of, though I don't claim it's scientific. The night *is* a strange time; things *are* different at night. And I think that at night—late at night—when the world is asleep, the boundary between *now* and *then* wavers. At certain moments and places it fades. I think that *there* in the darkness of the old Wister Post Office, in the dead of night, getting ready to mail my letter to Helen Worley in the old brass door of the letter drop—I think that I stood on one side of that slot in the year 1994, and that I dropped my letter, properly stamped, written and addressed in the ink and on the very paper of Helen Worley's youth, into the Brooklyn of 1882 on the other side of that worn old slot.

I believe that—because now, from that second secret little drawer, I took out the paper I found in it, opened it, and in rust-black ink on yellowing old paper I read:

Please, oh, please—who are you? Where can I reach you? Your letter arrived today, and I have wandered the house and garden ever since in an agony of excitement. I cannot conceive how you saw my letter in its secret place, but since you did, perhaps you will see this one too. Oh, tell me your letter is no hoax or cruel joke! Willy, if it is you—if you have discovered my letter and think to deceive your sister with a prank, I beg you to tell me! But if it is not—if I now address someone who has truly responded to my most secret hopes—do not for a moment longer keep me ignorant of who and where you are. For I, too—and I confess it willingly—long to see you! And I, too, feel, and am almost certain of it, that if I could know you, I would love you. It is impossible for me to think otherwise.

I must hear from you again. I shall not rest until I do.

I remain, most sincerely,
Helen Elizabeth Worley

After a long time, I opened the first little drawer of the old desk and took out the pen and ink I'd found there and a sheet of the notepaper.

For minutes, then, the pen in my hand, I sat there in the night staring down at the empty paper on the desk top. Finally, I dipped the pen into the old ink and wrote:

Helen, my dear:

I don't know how to say this so it will seem even comprehensible to you. But I do exist, here in Brooklyn, less than three blocks from where you now read this—in the year 1994. We are separated not by space but by the years that lie between us. Now I own the desk that you once had and at which you wrote the note I found in it. Helen, all I can tell you is that I answered that note, mailed it late at night at the old Wister Post Office, and that it somehow reached you, as I hope this will too.

This is no hoax! Can you imagine anyone playing a hoax that cruel? I live in Brooklyn within sight of your house, a Brooklyn that you cannot imagine. It is a city whose streets are now crowded with wheeled vehicles powered by engines. And it is a city extending far beyond the limits you know, with a population of millions, so crowded there is hardly room any longer for trees. From my window as I write, I can see—across the Brooklyn Bridge, which is hardly changed from the way you, too, can see it now—Manhattan Island, and rising from it are stone and steel buildings more than one thousand feet high.

You must believe me. I live. I exist, 112 years after you read this, and with the feeling that I have fallen in love with you.

I sat for some time staring at the wall, trying to figure out how to explain something I was certain was true. Then I wrote:

Helen: There are three secret drawers in our desk. Into the first you put only the letter I found. You cannot now add something to that drawer and hope that it will reach me. For I have already opened that drawer and found only the letter you put there. Nothing else can now come down through the years to me in that drawer, for you cannot now alter what you have already done.

Into the second drawer in 1882, you put the note that lies before me, which I found when I opened the drawer a few minutes ago. You put nothing else into it, and now that, too, cannot be changed.

But I haven't opened the third drawer, Helen. Not yet! It is the last way you can still reach me, and the last time. I will mail this as I did before, then wait. In a week I will open the last drawer.

Jake Belknap

It was a long week. I worked. I kept busy during the day. But at night I thought of hardly anything but the third secret drawer in my desk. I was terribly tempted to open it earlier, telling myself that whatever might lie in it had been put there many decades ago and must be there now. But I wasn't sure, and I waited.

Then, late at night, a week to the hour after I'd mailed my second letter at the old Wister Post Office, I pulled out the third drawer and reached in and took out the last little secret drawer that lay behind it. My hand was actually shaking, I couldn't bear to look directly—something was in the drawer—and I turned my head away. Then I looked.

I'd expected a long letter, very long, of many pages, and full of everything she wanted to say. But there was no letter at all. It was a photograph, about three inches square, faded brown in color, and with the photographer's name in tiny script down in the corner.

The photograph showed the head and shoulders of a young woman in a high-necked, dark dress, with a pin at the collar. Her dark hair was swept tightly back covering the ears in a style that is no longer in fashion. But neither the severe dress nor the hairstyle could spoil the beauty of the face that smiled out at me from that old photograph. It wasn't beautiful in any classic sense, I suppose. But it is the soft warm smile of her lips, and her eyes—large and serene as she looks out at me over the years—that make Helen Elizabeth Worley a beautiful woman.

Across the bottom of her photograph she had written, "I shall never forget you." And as I sat there at the old desk, staring at what she had written, I understood that, of course, that was the last time, as she knew, that she'd ever be able to reach me.

It wasn't the last time, though. There was one final way for Helen Worley to communicate with me over the years, and it took me a long time, as it must have taken her, to realize it.

Only a week ago, after much searching, I finally found it. It was late in the evening, and the sun was almost gone, when I found the old headstone in the cemetery, among the others stretching off in rows under the quiet trees. And then I read the inscription carved into the weathered old stone: *Helen Elizabeth Worley—1861–1934.* Under this were the words, **I NEVER FORGOT.**

And neither will I.

SELECTING DETAILS FROM THE STORY.
The following questions help you check your
reading comprehension. Put an *x* in the box
next to each correct answer.

1. The desk that Jake Belknap bought
   contained
   ☐ a. an old-fashioned stamp album.
   ☐ b. some letters from his folks in
      Florida.
   ☐ c. three secret drawers.

2. In her first letter, Helen Elizabeth Worley
   complained that the man she was going
   to marry
   ☐ a. was extremely poor.
   ☐ b. didn't take her seriously.
   ☐ c. wasn't handsome enough to suit her.

3. Jake mailed his letters to Helen
   ☐ a. by airmail.
   ☐ b. at a mailbox on the corner.
   ☐ c. at the Wister Post Office.

4. Jake found the final message from Helen
   ☐ a. on a headstone in the cemetery.
   ☐ b. attached to a photograph she
      sent him.
   ☐ c. in one of the compartments in
      the desk.

KNOWING NEW VOCABULARY WORDS. The
following questions check your vocabulary
skills. Put an *x* in the box next to each correct
answer.

1. Helen wrote her beloved: "I crave your
   bold glance, and I long for the tender
   warmth of your look!" The word *crave*
   means
   ☐ a. desire greatly.
   ☐ b. worry about.
   ☐ c. forget instantly.

2. Helen hoped that Jake's letter was not a
   hoax, or a cruel joke or prank. A *hoax* is a
   ☐ a. prize.
   ☐ b. message.
   ☐ c. trick.

3. Because the man she was engaged to was
   not sincere, Helen was angered and
   repelled by him. As used here, the word
   repelled means
   ☐ a. charmed.
   ☐ b. disgusted.
   ☐ c. amused.

4. She had a soft warm smile on her lips,
   and her eyes were large and serene. What
   is the meaning of the word *serene*?
   ☐ a. peaceful
   ☐ b. complaining
   ☐ c. closed

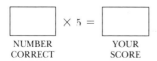

× 5 =	
NUMBER CORRECT	YOUR SCORE

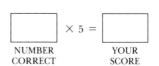

× 5 =	
NUMBER CORRECT	YOUR SCORE

IDENTIFYING STORY ELEMENTS. The following questions check your knowledge of story elements. Put an *x* in the box next to each correct answer.

1. Who is the *narrator* of "The Love Letter"?
   - ☐ a. Jake Belknap
   - ☐ b. Helen Elizabeth Worley
   - ☐ c. the proprietor of a secondhand store

2. What happened last in the *plot* of the story?
   - ☐ a. Jake walked to Brock Place to look for Helen's old house.
   - ☐ b. Jake found a photograph of a young woman in a high-necked, dark dress.
   - ☐ c. Jake put his hand into the opening of the desk and discovered the first secret drawer.

3. The story is *set* in
   - ☐ a. Brooklyn in 1994.
   - ☐ b. Manhattan in 1882.
   - ☐ c. a cemetery more than 100 years ago.

4. Because of the author's *style* of writing, "The Love Letter" may best be described as a
   - ☐ a. comedy.
   - ☐ b. detective story.
   - ☐ c. fantasy.

LOOKING AT CLOZE. The following questions use the cloze technique to check your reading comprehension. Complete the paragraph by filling in each blank with one of the words listed below. Each word appears in the story. Since there are five words and four blanks, one of the words will not be used.

When the Brooklyn Bridge was first

_____ in 1883, some called it
$_1$

"the eighth wonder of the world." The bridge,

which crosses over the East River, connects

the boroughs of Brooklyn and

_____ . It was designed by
$_2$

the engineer John A. Roebling, whose son

directed its _____ after the
$_3$

death of his father. The _____
$_4$

old bridge, 1,595 feet long, is a national

landmark in New York City.

population   Manhattan

construction

elegant   opened

☐ × 5 = ☐

NUMBER CORRECT   YOUR SCORE

☐ × 5 = ☐

NUMBER CORRECT   YOUR SCORE

LEARNING HOW TO READ CRITICALLY.
The following questions check your critical
thinking skills. Put an *x* in the box next to
each correct answer.

1. Clues in the story suggest that Jake
   Belknap and Helen Worley were both
   ☐ a. very happy with their lives.
   ☐ b. silly, fun-loving people.
   ☐ c. lonely and searching for happiness.

2. Jake probably put a stamp issued in 1869
   on the letter he wrote to Helen because
   ☐ a. that was the only stamp he could
       find.
   ☐ b. he intended the letter to travel far
       back in time.
   ☐ c. it seemed like an excellent way to
       get rid of the worthless old stamp.

3. Based on what Helen wrote in her first
   letter, we may infer that
   ☐ a. she had a good relationship with
       the man she was going to marry.
   ☐ b. the man she was going to marry did
       not treat her like an equal.
   ☐ c. she died of a broken heart at the
       age of thirty.

4. The most unusual thing about "The Love
   Letter" is that
   ☐ a. Jake Belknap was still a bachelor.
   ☐ b. Brooklyn changed so much over
       the years.
   ☐ c. characters who lived more than
       one hundred years apart seem able
       to communicate with each other.

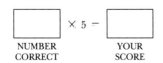

NUMBER   YOUR
CORRECT   SCORE

Improving Writing and Discussion Skills

- After he read Helen's first letter, Jake
  said that his "heart went out to her
  as I stared down at her secret, hopeless appeal against the world and time
  she lived in." What do Helen's words
  say about her—and about the world
  and time in which she lived?
- Why do you think the words "I never
  forgot" were written on Helen's
  headstone? Give reasons to support
  your opinion. Do you think Helen
  ever got married? Why? (Hint: think
  about the words on the headstone.)
- The author suggests that Jake and
  Helen fell in love with each other.
  Why do you think that happened?
  Is it possible to fall in love with a
  person you have never met? Explain.

Use the boxes below to total your scores
for the exercises. Then write your score on
pages 140 and 141.

☐ **S**ELECTING DETAILS FROM THE STORY
+
☐ **K**NOWING NEW VOCABULARY WORDS
+
☐ **I**DENTIFYING STORY ELEMENTS
+
☐ **L**OOKING AT CLOZE
+
☐ **L**EARNING HOW TO READ CRITICALLY
▼
☐ **S**core Total: Story 7

8. Fly Like an Eagle

by Elizabeth Van Steenwyk

Meet the Author

Elizabeth Van Steenwyk (1928–) was born in Galesburg, Illinois, and now lives in California. After graduating from Knox College, she worked for five years as a radio and TV producer before deciding to make writing her career. Van Steenwyk has written numerous children's books and more than one hundred short stories. One of her books, *The Best Horse*, was made into a motion picture of the same name.

I've never been this high off the ground in all my life, Angie thought, as she climbed the ladder to the ten-meter diving platform. I'm going to blow it, everything. I can't possibly jump 33 feet down to the water. Coach Hansen has to be crazy to think I'm going to dive from here. I won't . . . I can't do it.

"The first dive is petrifying from up there." Coach Hansen's voice came to her via microphone and loudspeaker and echoed through the dark empty swim stadium. He was seated in his favorite spot, halfway up on the right-hand side, Row M, Seat 56. He always sat there at every practice, to watch and to pronounce sentence, his voice leaping into the inky air of the building like an electronic kite with a tail of sound.

"You can do it, Angie. I know you can dive from there. It's time for you to move from springboard to platform."

No, I can't do it, Angie thought. And there's no way you're going to talk me into this dive, Coach Hansen!

She stood well back from the edge of the

platform, not even wanting to look down. Yet there was an insistent feeling of compulsion which drew her closer to the edge for a short, quick glimpse of the cool blue water below, waiting to swallow her.

"Come on, Angie. Time's wasting and you know you're going to jump."

Angie fluttered her arms and legs. She shook them again and again, as if wanting to be free of them.

"Think your dive through, Angie," Coach Hansen said. "Do it in your mind."

Leave me alone, Angie thought. I've done a front dive in this position a million times before on the three-meter. I know how to do it from down below, but *this* is different.

"Don't be ashamed to admit you're afraid," Coach Hansen said. "Fear is something we all have."

How would you know, Angie thought. When was the last time you stood up here?

"Let's analyze what it is you're afraid of." Coach Hansen's metallic voice droned on. "Is it fear of landing wrong? I don't think so. You've done that before from the three-meter and from the edge of the pool when you first began to dive. What is it then? Fear of getting the wind knocked out of you?"

Angie looked toward him, although she could see nothing but the rectangular brightness of the pool below. She shook her head no.

"Of course not. You're not afraid of that either. Then what is it?" the coach asked. He paused, dramatically Angie thought. Then he said, "I think I know. It's fear of the unknown. Is that what's bothering you?"

She nodded and a shiver ran uncontrollably through her body. Shakily she walked back to the farthest edge of the platform and wiped her hands on a towel.

Of course that's it, Hansen, she thought. Is that so hard to understand? I've never done this before, never felt the dive in my body going down from here, never felt the air rush over my skin nor felt gravity at this distance pulling my fingertips. Not from here. I can't dive from *here*.

"Your fear is perfectly normal," the coach's voice droned on without emotion. "It's not natural to want to dive from up there the first time. You need someone you have confidence in to push you."

I don't have any confidence in you, Angie thought. What gave you that idea? Right now, I don't think I even like you very much.

"You need someone to know when you're ready to do something you've never done before. I wouldn't let you dive if you weren't ready," Coach Hansen said.

Angie fluttered her arms and legs again. Then she shook her arms until they felt rubbery. She took a step toward the edge of the platform.

"Confidence will come from the dive itself," Coach Hansen said. "You've learned that with each new one. Now try it."

Angie stood at the edge, then put her toes in space and waited.

"It's just like the springboard," the coach said. "It's the same feeling once you're airborne. You have felt this dive before, Angie."

I wonder if I'm going to get sick and throw up, Angie thought. I've never done that from the ten-meter platform either.

"You may not believe it, but your body will know what to do once you're in the air," Coach Hansen said.

Angie didn't believe it—not for one second. She walked to the rear of the platform and dried her hands again. Then she turned and slowly took two steps toward the edge.

Her mouth felt so dry she knew she'd have to swallow the entire pool to make it feel wet again. She pulled at her suit and fluttered her arms.

"Look Angie, the thing you want most right now is to get this over with, right?"

Angie nodded. She couldn't have spoken, couldn't have uttered a sound.

"It will only take you two or three seconds to be down and out of the water on deck. Don't think. Just do it."

Angie flicked her wrists and heard her bones cracking in the stillness. She stood there, shaking inside until she was sure her blood must be frothy.

"What about all your plans for the AAU championship and the Olympics?" Coach Hansen asked.

So he's going to use that old trick on me is he, Angie thought, anger suddenly surging through her. Throwing the Olympics and the AAU at me like a trainer throws fish to his seals, as if I didn't know what he was doing. Does he think I'm dumb?

She walked back on the platform and looked down the steps, longing to use them.

Why did I ever want to do this? she thought miserably. Why couldn't I have played tennis like my sister or basketball like my brother? Why did I choose diving?

She remembered how it happened. Micki King, the Olympic gold medalist, had spoken at her Girl Scout district dinner when she was nine. She had listened intently as Micki related her exciting experiences and fantastic feelings about the sport. Right then Angie decided. She enrolled at the Y the next day and had shown so much early talent that her folks drove her special places for coaching. Then she had won every medal in sight and now that she was 15, everyone was talking

Olympics for her in four years. But that was crazy to think about with a coach as rotten as Hansen. How could she be ready by then?

"Okay, I've had it," the coach said. His voice sounded cold and hard. "Just walk down the steps and go home if you can't do this dive."

She threw him a murderous look. No, she thought. No, I won't! You aren't going to make a quitter out of me. She edged closer.

"That's better," the coach said softly. "Don't throw your body to fate now. Think it through, then dive."

She slapped a speck of grit from her left foot, dried her hands twice, and threw the towel down.

"You've got a dive inside you," Coach Hansen said. "Your muscles and nerves are programmed for it. There will come a moment when you know it will happen, Angie. At that moment, dive."

How long had he been coaching her? she thought. At least three years, and she'd heard that dozens of times before. Maybe it was time to find a new coach, someone who would say something different at least. Someone who might say something nice once in a while or be more understanding about her fear. Not this coach who treated her like a diving machine and only knew how to push and shove.

"Just remember to keep your body tightly controlled," he said. "If you're limp, that water will tear you apart. I want you to be as rigid as a nose cone in space."

A nose cone in space. That wasn't bad, Angie thought. He's getting better. Maybe if I keep him here long enough he'll write me a poem.

"Now think it through, Angie. You're just about ready, I know you are."

She turned to get the towel again, then thought, that's crazy. I keep drying my hands when I'm just going to get them wet in a second or two.

That's when she knew she was going to jump.

Now I'm just about ready, she thought. Just like he said. Angie stood at the edge and felt each muscle respond in anticipation as she thought the dive through from push-off to entry.

She'd known it all along, but Coach Hansen had to remind her. There is that moment when you know it's going to happen. There is that moment when training and reflexes take over. That moment is now.

Angie took a deep breath and pushed off, her body soaring into space. She spread her arms in the classic swan position and felt the air caress her body. For a lazy second Angie hung like a bird she had seen turning cartwheels in the sky. Fly like an eagle, she told herself. Fly. Then she felt her body begin its descent and her mind took total control. She brought her arms over her head and kept her body and legs straight as she pierced the water, scarcely causing a ripple. Angie stretched her dive downward before she curved back to the surface in a graceful arc.

"That wasn't bad, Angie," Coach Hansen said, as she pulled herself out of the water and toweled herself dry. "But you can do better. Go back up there and try it again."

"Right, Coach," she said. She grinned, feeling relieved and at ease with herself, as she headed for the ladder.

SELECTING DETAILS FROM THE STORY.
The following questions help you check your
reading comprehension. Put an *x* in the box
next to each correct answer.

1. At first, Angie refused to dive from the
   platform because she
   - ☐ a. wanted to embarrass her coach.
   - ☐ b. felt that she needed more practice.
   - ☐ c. had never jumped from that height
     before.

2. According to Coach Hansen, Angie's
   fear was
   - ☐ a. ridiculous.
   - ☐ b. amusing.
   - ☐ c. normal.

3. Angie had been coached by Hansen for
   - ☐ a. just a few months.
   - ☐ b. at least three years.
   - ☐ c. as long as she could remember.

4. As soon as Angie completed the dive,
   Coach Hansen
   - ☐ a. asked her to try it again.
   - ☐ b. told her she could leave.
   - ☐ c. said that it was the best dive he had
     ever seen.

KNOWING NEW VOCABULARY WORDS. The
following questions check your vocabulary
skills. Put an *x* in the box next to each correct
answer.

1. For a second Angie hung like a bird in
   the sky; then her body began its descent.
   As used here, the word *descent* means
   - ☐ a. moving downward.
   - ☐ b. rising swiftly.
   - ☐ c. shaking wildly.

2. After she heard Micki discuss how exciting
   diving was, Angie enrolled at the Y. The
   word *enrolled* means
   - ☐ a. forgot about.
   - ☐ b. signed up.
   - ☐ c. stayed away from.

3. Coach Hansen advised Angie to keep her
   body rigid and tightly controlled because
   the water "will tear you apart" if you're limp.
   What is the meaning of the word *rigid*?
   - ☐ a. chilly
   - ☐ b. stiff
   - ☐ c. bent over

4. His voice droned on without showing any
   feeling. Which expression best defines
   the word *droned*?
   - ☐ a. shouted and cheered
   - ☐ b. sang shrilly
   - ☐ c. spoke in the same boring way

☐ × 5 = ☐

NUMBER   YOUR
CORRECT   SCORE

☐ × 5 = ☐

NUMBER   YOUR
CORRECT   SCORE

IDENTIFYING STORY ELEMENTS. The following questions check your knowledge of story elements. Put an x in the box next to each correct answer.

1. Where is "Fly Like an Eagle" *set*?
   ☐ a. in a locker room
   ☐ b. at the Olympic Games
   ☐ c. in a swimming stadium

2. What happened last in the *plot* of the story?
   ☐ a. Coach Hansen told Angie to go home if she couldn't do the dive.
   ☐ b. Angie spread her arms and told herself to fly like an eagle.
   ☐ c. Angie climbed the ladder, thinking that she had never been so high off the ground before.

3. Identify the sentence that best expresses Angie's *inner conflict*.
   ☐ a. She wanted to dive but hesitated because she wasn't very graceful.
   ☐ b. She wanted to dive, but at the same time she was fearful of doing so.
   ☐ c. She didn't like her coach, nor did she have any confidence in him.

4. Which statement best tells the *theme* of "Fly Like an Eagle"?
   ☐ a. A young swimmer, aided by her coach, finally completes a challenging dive.
   ☐ b. A young swimmer refuses to be talked into making a dangerous dive.
   ☐ c. A coach is disappointed in the progress of a young swimmer.

	× 5 =	
NUMBER CORRECT		YOUR SCORE

LOOKING AT CLOZE. The following questions use the cloze technique to check your reading comprehension. Complete the paragraph by filling in each blank with one of the words listed below. Each word appears in the story. Since there are five words and four blanks, one of the words will not be used.

On August 6, 1926, an American swimmer named Gertrude Ederle became the first woman to _____ the English Channel. Her time of fourteen hours and thirty-one minutes broke the previous record by more than two hours, a _____ accomplishment. Ederle, a long-distance swimmer, held twenty world _____ at the time. She later became a swimming _____.

fantastic   coach

championships

swim   microphone

	× 5 =	
NUMBER CORRECT		YOUR SCORE

LEARNING HOW TO READ CRITICALLY.

The following questions check your critical thinking skills. Put an *x* in the box next to each correct answer.

1. The last sentence of the story suggests that Angie
   - ☐ a. was still afraid to dive.
   - ☐ b. lost faith in Coach Hansen.
   - ☐ c. conquered the fear she previously felt.

2. Based on what occurs in the story, we may conclude that Hansen was
   - ☐ a. a very poor coach.
   - ☐ b. a very fine coach.
   - ☐ c. thinking seriously about giving up coaching.

3. Which statement is true?
   - ☐ a. Coach Hansen often seemed to know what was going through Angie's mind.
   - ☐ b. From her spot high on the platform, Angie could hardly hear Coach Hansen's voice.
   - ☐ c. When Angie eventually decided to dive, Coach Hansen was surprised.

4. Angie's dive was quite good because she
   - ☐ a. stayed in the air for nearly five minutes.
   - ☐ b. kept her body and legs straight and scarcely caused a ripple when she hit the water.
   - ☐ c. hit the water with a loud, clear crash.

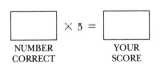

NUMBER CORRECT × 5 = YOUR SCORE

Improving Writing and Discussion Skills

- At one point during the story Angie thought that she didn't like Coach Hansen very much. Why did she feel that way? How do you think she felt about the coach at the end of the story? Support your opinion.
- Considering how long it took Angie to make the dive, why did Coach Hansen immediately tell her to dive again? Do you think that was the right thing for him to do? Explain.
- During the course of the story, Coach Hansen offered Angie at least ten different pieces of advice. List as many of these as you can. Which seemed to have the greatest effect on Angie? Explain your choice.

Use the boxes below to total your scores for the exercises. Then write your score on pages 140 and 141.

☐ SELECTING DETAILS FROM THE STORY
+
☐ KNOWING NEW VOCABULARY WORDS
+
☐ IDENTIFYING STORY ELEMENTS
+
☐ LOOKING AT CLOZE
+
☐ LEARNING HOW TO READ CRITICALLY
▼
☐ Score Total: Story 8

9. Don't Tread on Me

by Walter Dean Myers

Meet the Author

Walter Dean Myers (1937–) is one of today's best-known and most-honored writers of fiction for children and young adults. He has received a Council on Interracial Books for Children Award and a Newberry Honor. Myers has written more than two dozen novels. A number of these focus on the experiences of black teenagers in Harlem, New York City, where he lived for many years. "Don't Tread on Me" is from *Mojo and the Russians.*

The project at hand was teaching Major to talk. It was mainly my idea, but Kwami tried to take credit for it. After the problems we had had in trying to get the Russians to understand that we knew what they were up to, we had got into this big argument about communicating with other people. Kwami said that you could communicate with anything if you knew how to. He had read this article in an old issue of *New York* magazine where some people were teaching a monkey to talk. Now Kwami figured that a dog must be smarter than a monkey. I told him that I had learned in biology that monkeys were the next smartest things to people. He said that if monkeys were so smart how come they didn't live in apartments like dogs did. He said he saw a program about dogs once and that some dogs got a lot of money left to them when their owners died.

"Some of those dogs are millionaires," Kwami said. "I ain't no millionaire and I ain't never read about no monkey millionaire, either. Which is why I say that dogs is smarter than monkeys."

It didn't make a lot of book sense but it made a lot of seeing-is-believing sense. So when I thought about trying to teach Major to talk, I knew Kwami would go for the idea. As I said, he even tried to take credit for it.

We decided to take Major up to Leslie's house to teach him how to talk. The reason we decided to take him to Leslie's house was Leslie's grandmother stayed with them, and anytime you went to her house her grandmother would always come up with sandwiches or something.

Leslie had to go up first and make sure it was okay, and Kwami had to go home and tell his mother where he would be, and Judy took Major for a short walk while she was waiting for everyone to get ready. Anthony and Wayne were playing handball and that left me and Kitty on the stoop. Me and Kitty and the beginning of the worst day in my life. Or, if not the worst day, at least the most embarrassing moment.

Kitty had this book of word games she was doing. What you had to do was unscramble a word. Like LOTEH is HOTEL scrambled. So she was doing these and I was thinking about how she had held my hand that time in the park and how I really liked her. I was thinking about Judy having a picture of Kwami, too, and it all seemed pretty nice. So I asked Kitty if she wanted a picture of me.

"A picture of you?" She turned toward me real slow.

"Yeah." I was still feeling pretty good.

"What would I want a picture of you for?" she asked.

"Well, you could put it up on your wall or something," I said.

"Oh, I see," Kitty said. She was smiling a little and so I smiled a little, too. "And we could kind of be boy friend and girl friend."

"Yeah, kind of."

I was just about ready to figure out what picture I was going to give her when Kitty started laughing. She dropped her book and her pencil and really started to crack up. Then she rolled off the stoop and lay on the sidewalk. I never saw anybody laugh so hard. Wayne and Anthony came over and asked me what happened, and I said I didn't know. They tried to ask Kitty but she kept on laughing until the tears ran down her face. Finally she stopped enough to get back on the stoop and then she looked over at me and started laughing again until she was really crying.

Judy got back the same time that Leslie did. They asked Kitty what she was laughing about.

"This character wants me to . . ." She slapped her leg and started laughing again.

By this time I was really feeling bad because everyone was asking me why Kitty was laughing and naturally I didn't want to tell them.

"This character . . ." Kitty started telling what had happened again and was pointing at me.

"This character wants me to be his girl friend and hang his picture on my wall." Kitty finished just in time for more laughter to come out.

Wayne started laughing, and Anthony started laughing, and Leslie just kind of held her hand over her mouth and started giggling. I also knew that when Kwami got back I'd have to go through the whole thing all over again.

I was right. After they told him why Kitty was laughing, Kwami said, "When you people getting married, man?" Kwami and his big mouth.

Kwami put his hand on my shoulder and I pushed it off.

"Oh, I see, only Kitty can put her hand on your shoulder," he said. "I can understand that."

Then everybody started to crack up again. Now that's what I mean when I said I found out that I didn't understand Kwami. First he was all sad and everything about his mother and really seemed like he was okay.[1] Then the first chance he got he started cracking up on me because of that stupid thing I said to Kitty. We started up the stairs to Leslie's house and they were still on my case. I would have liked to punch out Kwami and Kitty right then and there. I really didn't think I was good enough to beat Kwami though— in fact, I was pretty sure that I wasn't. I had had a fight with Kitty about a year ago and it came out even, but she had gotten taller so I just tried to forget about the whole thing. At least when we started teaching Major to talk they got off me.

"The first thing we got to do," said Kwami, "is to decide what he's going to say."

"Seems to me that if he says anything he'll be just about the coolest dog in the world," Kitty said.

" 'Cause he's not a puppy, see?" Kwami lifted Major's chin slightly and looked at the dog as he spoke. "If he was a puppy you could

teach him to say anything because he couldn't know any better. But he knows a lot of things, now, so you got to be careful. Say you try to teach him to ask for a piece of fried chicken and he don't like fried chicken. He might not say anything just because he don't like what you're trying to teach him to say, dig?"

"Suppose he don't speak English?" Wayne asked.

"Don't be dumb, Wayne. American dogs all understand American and that's what we're going to teach Major to speak." Kwami gave Wayne a mean look. "And if you come up with one more dumb statement I'm going to wait till the next time it rains and then turn your nose upside down and drown you."

"So what are we going to teach Major to say?" I asked.

"Something patriotic," Kwami said. "So he'll feel good saying it."

"How about 'Give me liberty or give me death'?"

"He might think we're trying to bump him off."

"How about, 'I regret that I have only one life—' "

"There you go with that dying stuff again," said Kwami.

"All that good patriotic stuff is about being dead or how you gonna die if something don't happen." Wayne was beginning to whine. Wayne always whined when somebody got on him.

"How about 'tip-a-canoe and Tyler too'?"[2]

"What's that mean?"

---

1. This is a reference to the fact that Kwami's mother was ill.

2. **"Tippecanoe and Tyler too"**: a campaign slogan used by William Henry Harrison and his running mate, John Tyler, in 1840. Harrison's victory over the Shawnee Indians at the Battle of Tippecanoe helped him win the presidency.

"I don't know. But it's got to be famous 'cause we learned it in history."

"The only thing you got to be to be famous in history is dead a bunch of years."

"I have it. How about 'Don't tread on me'?"[3]

That was the famous American saying that we decided we would teach Major. The first thing that we did was to write the words on four large pieces of paper. Then Kwami and Kitty took turns reading the words to Major as Judy held him in her arms.

"Don't," Kwami said. He looked at Major and the dog seemed to understand him.

"Tread." Major still looked at Kwami.

"On." Major's tail began to wag.

"Me." Major squirmed.

"Now comes the hard part," Kitty said.

"You meaning getting my main dog here to talk?"

"No, just getting him to try," Kitty answered. "Dogs have been treated so badly over the years that they don't even try to talk. People usually just tell them to do things like sit down, and heel, and play dead, or get off the sidewalk that that's what they think they're supposed to be doing. We got to convince Major that he's really supposed to talk."

"Leave that to the big K," Kwami said. "Kwami Green, teacher of frogs and dogs. Kwami Green, teacher supreme. Not only will I have your frog hopping, I'll get his foot to pattin' and not only will your dog talk, he'll speak Pig Latin."

"Don't be telling us that jive, tell Major," Judy said.

Kwami knelt down in front of Major and looked him right in the eye.

"Not only can you talk if you want to, Major, but you can converse on any level on which you choose. Now, dig, watch Kwami's lips as he speaks and then you repeat after me. Don't feel self-conscious if you don't get it right the first time 'cause I got until nearly three o'clock to get you together. Now, repeat after me: Don't. . . . tread. . . . on. . . . me."

Major just looked at Kwami and wagged his tail.

Kwami got a little closer to Major until their noses were almost touching. "Look into my eyes and believe you can talk, dog," Kwami said. "I'm not teaching you anything jive to say. I'm teaching you some good stuff. This is a famous American saying. Now, I'm going to lift my head a little so you can watch my lips. See." Kwami lifted his head so that Major could see his lips. "Now repeat after me." Kwami moved his lips in slow, exaggerated movements as he repeated the phrase. "Don't . . . tread . . . on . . . me!"

Major barked once.

"I think he got it!" Kwami said.

"All he said was woof!"

"He's warming up," Kwami said. "Give him a little time. What's the first thing that you said when you started talking, turkey? You probably couldn't even say woof."

"Don't . . . tread . . . on . . . me!"

Major got closer to Kwami and licked him on the mouth. Kwami didn't move.

"Oh, sweat!" Wayne said. "Major kissed Kwami right on the lips and Kwami didn't even move."

"I can't reject him at this crucial point, man," Kwami said, but he looked a bit uncomfortable. "That would be like leaving a kid back in kindergarten.

"Don't . . . tread . . . on . . . me!"

Major licked Kwami's face again.

"I think Major's in love with Kwami."

---

3. **"Don't tread on me"**: motto of the first official American flag.

Judy grinned. "And by the way Kwami is taking his kisses, I think we may have something going."

"That's what's wrong with you people." Kwami jumped up. "Anytime you try to do something serious you people start clowning around. You don't know nothing about no psychology or nothing. I give up."

Kwami sat down on a hassock and ate one of the grilled cheese sandwiches Leslie's grandmother had made. It was obvious that he was mad.

"Don't get upset, Kwami," Kitty said. "Maybe it just takes awhile. We'll try again some other time."

"He might be ready to talk now," Judy said, "and just waiting for the right time. I know a woman who had a little boy who didn't talk until he was almost seven years old and then he just started talking one day like he had been talking all along."

"That's right," Leslie added. "I've heard of that kind of thing happening myself. He may get up in the middle of the night and start talking."

"You know, I was thinking," I said. "Maybe you made more progress than you think you did."

"What do you mean?" asked Kwami.

"Well, what's the saying you were trying to teach him?"

"Don't tread on me," answered Kwami.

"Well, he didn't tread on you, did he?"

Kwami just sighed.

That night I got home and my father was all set to have one of his "meaningful"

conversations with me. We had one about twice a month. He usually gets on this real calm attitude and asks me something like what I thought of the crises in South Africa, or the environment issue, or some other good doing thing like that. Only halfway through my answer, he would interrupt to tell me what he thought and that would be the end of the conversation. I'd sit there and listen until he was satisfied, then it would be over. Sometimes, just to be different, he would start the conversation off by asking me what I did that day. Then he would tell me what I should have been doing to better myself and what he would have been doing if he had been me. Then he'd watch television until he fell asleep in his chair.

This was one of those days when he was asking about what I did during the day so I told him about trying to teach Major to talk.

"Trying to do what?" he asked.

"Trying to teach Major to talk," I repeated.

"Okay." He nodded his head up and down, but I knew he didn't believe a word I was saying. "Major is that little blond girl's dog, isn't he?"

"Yep," I said, really enjoying the fact that he didn't know what was going on.

"Well, okay," he said, switching on the television. "I guess you know what you're doing. By the way, there's something on your dresser for you. It was pushed under the door."

On the dresser was a white envelope with my name on it. Inside the envelope was a picture of Kitty. On the back it said "to my friend, Dean." Things were looking up.

SELECTING DETAILS FROM THE STORY.
The following questions help you check your
reading comprehension. Put an *x* in the box
next to each correct answer.

1. When Dean suggested that he and Kitty
   be boyfriend and girlfriend, Kitty
   ☐ a. agreed at once.
   ☐ b. said she would think about it.
   ☐ c. burst out laughing.

2. The reason everyone went to Leslie's
   house was that
   ☐ a. it was closest.
   ☐ b. it has the most room.
   ☐ c. Leslie's grandmother always made
        sandwiches or something similar.

3. Eventually Kwami and the others decided
   to teach Major to say
   ☐ a. "tip-a-canoe and Tyler too."
   ☐ b. "Don't tread on me."
   ☐ c. "Give me liberty or give me death."

4. Dean said that his father sometimes asked
   him what he did during the day in order to
   ☐ a. use the opportunity to give
        Dean advice.
   ☐ b. praise Dean.
   ☐ c. find out who Dean's friends were.

KNOWING NEW VOCABULARY WORDS. The
following questions check your vocabulary
skills. Put an *x* in the box next to each correct
answer.

1. He said, "Leave that to . . . Kwami Green,
   teacher of frogs and dogs. Kwami Green,
   teacher supreme." As used here, the word
   supreme means
   ☐ a. modest.
   ☐ b. likable.
   ☐ c. greatest.

2. To teach the dog, Kwami moved his lips
   in slow, exaggerated movements as he
   repeated the words. Movements that are
   exaggerated are very
   ☐ a. small.
   ☐ b. large.
   ☐ c. pleasant.

3. Kwami said, "Not only can you talk if you
   want to, Major, but you can converse on
   any level on which you choose." As used
   in this sentence, the word *converse* means
   ☐ a. hold a conversation.
   ☐ b. argue loudly.
   ☐ c. refuse to speak.

4. He was especially careful not to upset the
   dog at the crucial moment. The word
   crucial means
   ☐ a. very important.
   ☐ b. meaningless.
   ☐ c. next to last.

	× 5 =	
NUMBER CORRECT		YOUR SCORE

	× 5 =	
NUMBER CORRECT		YOUR SCORE

IDENTIFYING STORY ELEMENTS. The following questions check your knowledge of story elements. Put an *x* in the box next to each correct answer.

1. What happened first in the *plot* of the story?
   - ☐ a. Dean found an envelope with a picture of Kitty inside it.
   - ☐ b. Major kissed Kwami.
   - ☐ c. Dean told his father about trying to teach Major to talk.

2. Which statement best *characterizes* Kwami?
   - ☐ a. He often spoke with an air of confidence and was eager to take charge.
   - ☐ b. He was timid, soft-spoken, and shy.
   - ☐ c. Although he was younger than any of his friends, he was the tallest and strongest.

3. The *mood* of "Don't Tread on Me" is
   - ☐ a. serious and solemn.
   - ☐ b. very suspenseful.
   - ☐ c. light and amusing.

4. Which was the author's *purpose* in writing the story?
   - ☐ a. to teach the reader an important lesson
   - ☐ b. to amuse or entertain the reader
   - ☐ c. to shock or frighten the reader

LOOKING AT CLOZE. The following questions use the cloze technique to check your reading comprehension. Complete the paragraph by filling in each blank with one of the words listed below. Each word appears in the story. Since there are five words and four blanks, one of the words will not be used.

Born in 1736, the American

_____ Patrick Henry gained
                1

fame as a fiery speaker. Governor of Virginia

during the Revolutionary War, Henry is

probably best remembered for his stirring

words: "Give me _____ or give
                      2

me death!" He uttered these words in 1775

in a call for the colonies to arm themselves

against the _____ . After leaving
                3

public service, Henry became one of the most

distinguished and _____ lawyers
                        4

of his day.

liberty   conversations

famous

English   patriot

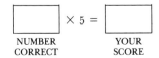

NUMBER   YOUR
CORRECT   SCORE

⬜ × 5 = ⬜

NUMBER   YOUR
CORRECT   SCORE

LEARNING HOW TO READ CRITICALLY.
The following questions check your critical
thinking skills. Put an *x* in the box next to
each correct answer.

1. Judging by what occurs and is said in the
   story, we may conclude that several of
   the youngsters
   ☐ a. hardly knew each other.
   ☐ b. went to different schools.
   ☐ c. had a good sense of humor.

2. Which statement is true?
   ☐ a. Teaching Major to talk was mainly
       Kwami's idea.
   ☐ b. At first, Kwami seemed certain
       that he would be able to teach Major
       to talk.
   ☐ c. Major actually succeeded in saying
       two words.

3. Clues in story suggest that
   ☐ a. Kwami didn't possess as much
       patience as he thought he had.
   ☐ b. Kwami actually made a good deal
       of progress in teaching Major to talk.
   ☐ c. Major will probably begin to start
       talking one day.

4. When Dean saw the picture that Kitty had
   sent him, he probably felt
   ☐ a. foolish.
   ☐ b. annoyed.
   ☐ c. delighted.

	× 5 =	
NUMBER CORRECT		YOUR SCORE

Improving Writing and Discussion Skills

- When Kwami became upset over
  his failure to teach Major to talk,
  Dean suggested that Kwami had
  made more progress than he thought.
  "What do you mean?" asked Kwami.
  "Well, he didn't tread on you, did he?"
  said Dean. Was Dean trying to make
  Kwami feel better—or was Dean
  teasing Kwami? Explain.
- "Don't Tread on Me" contains
  humorous dialogue, amusing
  expressions, and a comical situation.
  Support this statement by referring
  to the story.
- At the end of the story Dean found
  a picture of Kitty. Why do you think
  Kitty made fun of Dean when he first
  asked her for her picture?

Use the boxes below to total your scores
for the exercises. Then write your score on
pages 140 and 141.

	SELECTING DETAILS FROM THE STORY
+	
	KNOWING NEW VOCABULARY WORDS
+	
	IDENTIFYING STORY ELEMENTS
+	
	LOOKING AT CLOZE
+	
	LEARNING HOW TO READ CRITICALLY
▼	
	Score Total: Story 9

10. The Sentimentality of William Tavener

by Willa Cather

Meet the Author

Willa Cather (1873–1947) is recognized as
one of the leading fiction writers of the
twentieth century. Born in Virginia, Cather
moved to Nebraska with her family when she
was ten years old. After attending the University
of Nebraska, Cather authored twelve novels and
fifty-eight short stories, and won a Pulitzer Prize
for literature. Her best-known works, *Death Comes
for the Archbishop, O Pioneers!,* and *My Antonia,*
are about the American Southwest.

*I*t takes a strong woman to make any
sort of success of living in the West. Hester
undoubtedly was that. When people spoke
of William Tavener as the most prosperous
farmer in McPherson County, they usually
added that his wife was a "good manager."
She was strong-willed, quick of tongue, and
very capable. The only reason her husband
did not consult her about his business was
that she did not *wait* to be consulted.

It would have been impossible for William
to follow all of Hester's advice, but he usually
acted on some of her suggestions. When she
continually criticized the "wastefulness"
of letting a new threshing machine stand
unprotected in the open, he eventually built
a shed for it. When she ridiculed his plan
for building a corral made of earth walls

87

to fence in the hogs, he insisted on starting the structure. But in the end he went off quietly to town and bought enough barbed wire to complete the job. When the first heavy rains came, the pigs knocked down the earth wall and climbed out over it. Later, at dinner, Hester teasingly told the story of the little pig that built a mud house. But William did not smile and remained serious. Silence, indeed, was William's refuge and his strength.

William set his boys a good example to respect their mother. People who knew him very well realized just how much he admired her. But he was a stubborn man to his neighbors, and even to his sons. He was difficult, determined, and very thrifty.

There was an occasional blue day around the house when William went over the bills, but he never objected to items related to his wife's purchases. As a result, many of the little things that Hester bought for her boys she charged to her personal account.

One spring night Hester sat in a rocking chair by the living room window, darning socks. She rocked back and forth violently, moving her needle with agitation. It took only a casual glance to see that she was very worked up about something. William sat on the other side of the table calmly reading his paper. If he had noticed that his wife was upset, his faced showed no sign of it. He must have heard the sarcastic tone of her remarks at the supper table, and he must have noticed the moody silence of the two older boys as they ate. He must have seen Billy, the younger boy, suddenly push back his plate when supper was only half over and slip away from the table, trying to hold back tears. But William Tavener never paid attention to threatening clouds in the domestic skies, and

he never looked for a storm until it broke.

After supper the boys had gone to the pond under the willows to get rid of the dust of plowing. Hester could hear an occasional splash and a laugh ringing through the stillness of the night as she sat by the open window.

She sat silently for almost an hour reviewing in her mind many plans of attack. But Hester was too active a person to be much of a planner, and she usually came straight to the point. At last she cut her thread and suddenly put down her darning needle. "William," she said sharply, "I don't think it would hurt you to let the boys go to that circus in town tomorrow."

William continued to read his paper, but it was not Hester's custom to wait for an answer. She usually guessed his arguments and attacked them one by one before he made them.

"You've been short of hands all summer, and you've worked the boys hard. A man ought to use his own flesh and blood as well as he does his hired hands. We're plenty able to afford it, and it's little enough that our boys ever spend. I don't see how you can expect 'em to be steady and hard working unless you encourage 'em a little. I could never see much harm in circuses, and our boys have never been to one. Oh, I know the Howley boys get wild and carry on when they go, but our boys ain't that sort, an' you know it, William. The animals are real educational, an' our boys don't get to see much out here on the prairie. It was different where we were raised, but the boys have got no advantages here. If you don't take care, they'll grow up to be ignorant."

Hester paused for a moment, and William folded up his paper, but uttered no remark. His sisters in Virginia had often said that only a quiet man like William could ever have lived with Hester Perkins. Secretly, William was rather proud of his wife's "gift of speech," and of the fact that at a meeting she could speak as smoothly as anyone there. He himself tended to say very little.

"Nobody was ever hurt by goin' to a circus. Why, I remember I went to one myself, when I was little. I had almost forgotten about it. It was over at Newton, and I remember how I had my heart set on going. I don't think I'd ever have forgiven my father if he hadn't taken me, though that red clay road was in terrible shape after the rains."

Hester paused, then went on. "I remember that they had an elephant and six parrots, a Rocky Mountain lion, a cage of monkeys, an' two camels. My, but they were a sight to me then!"

Hester shook her head and smiled at the recollection. She was not expecting a response from William yet, so she was startled when he said in a very serious voice, "No, there was only one camel. The other was a dromedary."

She looked at him closely.

"Why, William, how could you know that?"

William folded his paper and answered with some hesitation, "I was there, too."

Hester's interest flashed up. "Well, I never! William! To think of my finding this out after all those years! Why, you couldn't have been much older than our Billy then. It seems strange I never saw you when you was little, to remember anything about you. But then, you folks from Back Creek never had anything to do with us Gap people. But how come you got to go? Your father was stricter with you than you are with our boys."

"I reckon I shouldn't a' gone," he said slowly, "but boys will do foolish things. I had done a good deal of fox hunting the winter before, and father let me keep the money I earned. I hired Tom Smith's boy to weed the cornfield for me, an' then I slipped off without Father knowin' it an' went to the show."

Hester spoke up warmly. "Well, there, William! It didn't do you any harm, I guess. You always worked so hard, it must have been a great treat for a little fellow. That clown must have just tickled you to death."

William crossed his knees and leaned back in his chair.

"I reckon I could tell all of that fool's jokes now. Sometimes I can't help thinkin' about 'em when the village meeting runs on too long. I remember that I had on a new pair of boots that hurt me something fierce, but I forgot all about 'em when that clown rode the donkey. I recall I had to take them boots off as soon as I got out of sight of the town, and walked home barefoot in the mud."

"Poor little fellow!" Hester exclaimed, drawing her chair nearer and leaning her elbows on the table. "What uncomfortable shoes for children they used to make then. I remember I went up to Back Creek to see the circus wagons go by on their way down from Romney. The circus people stopped at the creek to water the animals, and the elephant got stubborn an' broke a big limb off the willow tree that grew by the Scribners' porch. The Scribners were afraid as death he'd pull the house down. But this much I saw him do: he waded in the creek and filled his trunk with water and squirted it in through the window and nearly ruined Ellen Scribner's pink dress that she had just ironed and set out on the bed to wear to the circus."

"I reckon that must have been a bother to Ellen," chuckled William, "for she was mighty prim in them days."

Hester drew her chair still nearer to William's. Since the children had begun growing up, her conversation with her husband had been confined almost completely to matters concerning expenses. Over the years their relationship had increasingly become a business one. In her desire to obtain a little bit more for her boys, she had, without realizing it, taken an almost hostile attitude toward her husband. She argued doggedly with William on behalf of her sons. The struggle had gone on for so long, it had almost crowded out the memory of a closer relationship. This sharing of thoughts tonight, when common recollections took them unaware, opened their hearts and had all the miracle of romance.

They talked on and on: of old neighbors, of old familiar faces in the valley where they had grown up, of long forgotten incidents of their youth—weddings, picnics, sleighing parties, holidays. For years they had talked of nothing else but butter and eggs and the price of such things. And now they had much to say to each other as people who meet after a long separation.

When the clock struck ten, William rose and went over to his walnut desk and unlocked it. From his red leather wallet he took out a ten-dollar bill and placed it on the table next to Hester.

"Tell the boys not to stay late at the circus, 'an not to drive the horses hard," he said quietly, and went off to bed.

Hester blew out the lamp and sat still in the dark for a long time. She left the bill lying on the table where William had placed it.

She had a painful sense of having missed something, or lost something. She felt that somehow the years had cheated her.

The little locust trees that grew by the fence were white with blossoms. Their sweet aroma floated out to her on the night wind. She remembered a night long ago, when the first whippoorwill of the spring was heard, and the rough girls of Hawkins Gap had held her laughing and struggling under the locust tree. They had searched her for a lock of her sweetheart's hair, which every girl is supposed to have when the first whippoorwill sings. Two of those same girls had been her bridesmaids. Hester had been a very happy bride.

She rose and went quietly into the bedroom. William was sleeping heavily, but occasionally he moved his hand over his face to ward off the flies. Hester went into the parlor and took a piece of mosquito net from a basket there. She went back to the bedroom and spread the net over William's face. Then she sat down by the bed and listened to his deep, regular breathing until she heard the boys returning. She went out to meet them and to warn them not to waken their father.

"I'll be up early to get your breakfast, boys. Your father says you can go to the circus."

As she handed the money to the eldest, she felt a sudden throb of allegiance to her husband. "You be careful with that," she said sharply, "an' don't waste it. Your father works hard for his money."

The boys looked at each other in astonishment and suddenly felt that they had lost a powerful ally.

SELECTING DETAILS FROM THE STORY. The following questions help you check your reading comprehension. Put an *x* in the box next to each correct answer.

1. When Hester offered her husband advice, he usually
   - ☐ a. ignored whatever she suggested.
   - ☐ b. followed all of her suggestions at once.
   - ☐ c. acted on some of her suggestions.

2. Hester thought that it would be a good idea to
   - ☐ a. let the boys go to the circus in town.
   - ☐ b. build a corral made out of earth.
   - ☐ c. let the threshing machine stand unprotected in the open for a while.

3. William knew all about the circus Hester had gone to because
   - ☐ a. she had told him about it many times.
   - ☐ b. he had read about it in the local newspaper.
   - ☐ c. he had been there too.

4. Over the years, Hester's conversations with her husband had been mainly about
   - ☐ a. business matters.
   - ☐ b. incidents that took place during their youth.
   - ☐ c. how to provide their children with the best possible education.

KNOWING NEW VOCABULARY WORDS. The following questions check your vocabulary skills. Put an *x* in the box next to each correct answer.

1. William Tavener was a very successful and prosperous farmer. What is the meaning of the word *prosperous*?
   - ☐ a. lazy
   - ☐ b. wealthy
   - ☐ c. unfortunate

2. Worked up about something, Hester rocked back and forth in the chair violently, moving with agitation. As used here, the word *agitation* means feeling
   - ☐ a. disturbed or upset.
   - ☐ b. unusually calm.
   - ☐ c. greatly appreciated.

3. William thought that Ellen must have been very annoyed when the elephant squirted water on her dress, for she was "mighty prim" in those days. Which of the following best defines the word *prim*?
   - ☐ a. careless
   - ☐ b. neat
   - ☐ c. popular

4. Hester had argued doggedly with her husband on behalf of her sons. The word *doggedly* means
   - ☐ a. scarcely.
   - ☐ b. foolishly.
   - ☐ c. stubbornly.

	× 5 =	
NUMBER CORRECT		YOUR SCORE

	× 5 =	
NUMBER CORRECT		YOUR SCORE

91

IDENTIFYING STORY ELEMENTS. The following questions check your knowledge of story elements. Put an *x* in the box next to each correct answer.

1. Where is "The Sentimentality of William Tavener" *set*?
   □ a. in a house somewhere in the West
   □ b. on a farm in the South
   □ c. at a circus in a small town

2. Which group of words best *characterizes* Hester?
   □ a. strong willed; well spoken; capable
   □ b. determined; boastful; wasteful
   □ c. quiet; thoughtful; shy

3. Identify the statement that best illustrates *character development*.
   □ a. When William refused to permit the boys to go to the circus, they responded with a moody silence.
   □ b. At the beginning of the story Hester was very upset with her husband; at the end of the story she felt an allegiance to him.
   □ c. At the beginning of the story the boys hoped to go to the circus; at the end of the story they were allowed to go.

4. What happened last in the *plot* of the story?
   □ a. William explained how he went to the circus years ago.
   □ b. The boys went swimming in the pond.
   □ c. Hester gave her son a ten-dollar bill.

```
┌──────┐        ┌──────┐
│      │ × 5 =  │      │
└──────┘        └──────┘
NUMBER          YOUR
CORRECT         SCORE
```

LOOKING AT CLOZE. The following questions use the cloze technique to check your reading comprehension. Complete the paragraph by filling in each blank with one of the words listed below. Each word appears in the story. Since there are five words and four blanks, one of the words will not be used.

More than two thousand years ago the ancient Romans held _____ in huge outdoor arenas. The most famous of these was the Circus Maximus, an enormous _____ that seated well over one hundred thousand spectators. The spectacular chariot race was _____ the most popular event at the circus. The horses, each pulling a chariot, had to _____ seven laps around the track.

structure   **circuses**

undoubtedly

consulted   **complete**

```
┌──────┐        ┌──────┐
│      │ × 5 =  │      │
└──────┘        └──────┘
NUMBER          YOUR
CORRECT         SCORE
```

92

LEARNING HOW TO READ CRITICALLY.
The following questions check your critical thinking skills. Put an *x* in the box next to each correct answer.

1. William Tavener "never paid attention to threatening clouds in the domestic skies, and he never looked for a storm until it broke." This means that William
   - ☐ a. didn't heed problems at home until they finally couldn't be ignored any longer.
   - ☐ b. always hoped for favorable weather.
   - ☐ c. neglected to fix the roof of his house until it started to leak.

2. Clues in the story suggest that Hester Tavener
   - ☐ a. didn't care very much about her children.
   - ☐ b. contributed greatly to her husband's success.
   - ☐ c. disliked living on a farm.

3. Following her long conversation with William, Hester had "a painful sense of having missed something, or lost something." Hester probably realized that she
   - ☐ a. had forgotten where she put the ten-dollar bill.
   - ☐ b. and William could have shared many similar experiences.
   - ☐ c. and William had an ideal relationship.

4. Hester placed a mosquito net over William's face because she
   - ☐ a. didn't want to look at him.
   - ☐ b. was bothered by his snoring.
   - ☐ c. cared about his comfort.

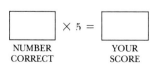

NUMBER CORRECT × 5 = YOUR SCORE

Improving Writing and Discussion Skills

- Although Hester and William were both strong-minded individuals, there was also a soft side to each character's nature. Find evidence in the story to support this statement. (Note that the word *sentimentality* in the title means "having tender feelings.")
- According to the author, the unusual evening that Hester and William spent together "had all the miracle of romance." Why do you think the author used the word *miracle*? Why did she use the word *romance*?
- At the end of the story, the boys suddenly felt that they had lost a powerful ally. Why? Refer to dialogue in the story when you answer the question.

Use the boxes below to total your scores for the exercises. Then write your score on pages 140 and 141.

☐ **S**ELECTING DETAILS FROM THE STORY
+
☐ **K**NOWING NEW VOCABULARY WORDS
+
☐ **I**DENTIFYING STORY ELEMENTS
+
☐ **L**OOKING AT CLOZE
+
☐ **L**EARNING HOW TO READ CRITICALLY
▼
☐ **S**core Total: Story 10

II. Say It with Flowers

by Toshio Mori

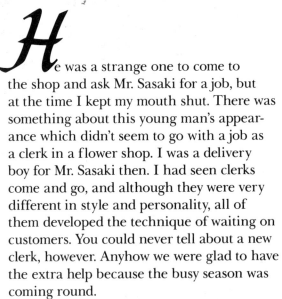

*H*e was a strange one to come to the shop and ask Mr. Sasaki for a job, but at the time I kept my mouth shut. There was something about this young man's appearance which didn't seem to go with a job as a clerk in a flower shop. I was a delivery boy for Mr. Sasaki then. I had seen clerks come and go, and although they were very different in style and personality, all of them developed the technique of waiting on customers. You could never tell about a new clerk, however. Anyhow we were glad to have the extra help because the busy season was coming round.

Mr. Sasaki probably remembered last year's rush when Tommy, Mr. Sasaki, and I had to do everything and had too many different things to do at one time. He wanted to be ready this time.

"Another clerk and we'll be all set for any kind of business," Mr. Sasaki used to tell us. So when Teruo came around looking for a job, he got it, and Morning Glory Flower Shop

Meet the Author

Toshio Mori (1910–1980) has written hundreds of stories, most of which reflect his background and experiences as a Japanese American. Mori grew up in San Leandro, California, where for many years he worked in a flower shop owned by his brother. That provided the inspiration for "Say It with Flowers." The story was published in his first collection, *Yokohama, California*, which deals with life in San Leandro and Oakland.

was all set for the year as far as our boss was concerned.

When Teruo reported for work the following morning, Mr. Sasaki introduced him to Tommy. Tommy had been our number one clerk for a long time.

"Tommy, teach him all you can," Mr. Sasaki said. "Teruo's going to be with us from now on."

"Sure," Tommy said.

"Tommy's a good florist. You watch and listen to him," the boss told the young man.

"All right, Mr. Sasaki," the young man said. He turned to us and said, "My name is Teruo." We shook hands.

We got to know one another pretty well after that. He was a quiet fellow with very little words for anybody, but his smile charmed a person. We soon learned that he knew nothing about the florist business. He could identify a rose when he saw one, and gardenias and carnations too, but other flowers and gardening materials were new to him.

"You fellows teach me something about this business and I'll be grateful. I want to start from the bottom," Teruo said.

Tommy eagerly went about showing Teruo the florist trade. Every morning for several days Tommy went over the prices of the flowers with him. He told Teruo what to do on telephone orders, how to keep the greens and flowers fresh, and how to make bouquets. "You need a little more time to learn how to make a funeral display," Tommy said. "That'll come later."

In a couple of weeks Teruo was just as good a clerk as we had had in a long time. He was eager to learn and was a very hard worker. It was about this time that our boss decided to take his yearly business trip to Seattle. He was satisfied with Teruo, and he knew we could get along without him for a while. He went off and left Tommy in charge.

During Mr. Sasaki's absence I was often in the shop helping Tommy and Teruo with the customers and the orders. One day he asked me, "How can you tell when a flower is fresh and when it's old? I can't tell one from the other. All I do is follow your instructions and sell the ones you tell me to sell first, but I can't tell one from the other."

I laughed. "You don't need to know that, Teruo," I told him. "When the customers ask you whether the flowers are fresh, just say firmly, 'Yes! Our flowers are always fresh!' "

Teruo picked up a vase of carnations. "These flowers came in four or five days ago, didn't they?" he asked me.

"You're right. Five days ago," I said.

"How long will they last if a customer bought them today?" Teruo asked.

"I guess in this weather they'll keep a day or two," I said.

"Then they're *old*," Teruo almost gasped. "Why, we have fresh ones that last a week or so in the shop."

"Sure, Teruo. But why should you worry about that?" Tommy said. "Just talk convincingly to the customers and they'll believe you. 'Are our flowers always fresh? You bet they are! They just came in a little while ago from the market!' "

Teruo looked at us calmly. "That's a hard thing to say when you know it isn't true."

"You'll get used to it sooner or later," I told him. "Everybody has to do it. You too, unless you want to lose your job."

"I don't think I can say it convincingly again," Teruo said. "I must've said yes forty times already when I didn't know any better. It'll be harder next time."

"You've said it forty times already," said Tommy, "so why can't you say it forty million times more? What's the difference? Remember, Teruo, it's your business to live."

"I don't like it," said Teruo.

"Do we like it? Do you think we're any different from you?" Tommy asked Teruo. "You're just a new kid. You don't know any better so I don't get sore, but you got to play the game when you're in it. You understand, don't you?"

Teruo nodded. For a moment he stood and looked curiously at us. Then he went away to water the plants.

In the following weeks we watched Teruo develop into a fine salesclerk, except for one thing. When a customer forgot to ask about the condition of the flowers Teruo did splendidly. But if someone asked about the freshness of the flowers, he would look uncomfortable and would sometimes sputter or would stand gaping speechlessly. Occasionally, looking embarrassed, he would take the customers to the fresh flowers in the rear of the store and complete the sales there.

"Don't do that anymore, Teruo," Tommy warned him one afternoon. "Don't sell the fresh flowers in the back when we got plenty of the old stuff in the front. We can't throw all that stuff away. First thing you know the boss'll start losing money and we'll all be thrown out."

"I wish I could sell like you," Teruo said. "But whenever they ask me, 'Is this fresh?' 'How long will it keep?' I begin to forget about selling the stuff, and begin to think about the difference between the fresh flowers and the old ones. Then the trouble begins."

"Remember, the boss has to run the shop to make money so he can keep it going," Tommy told him. "When he returns next week you better not let him see you sell the fresh flowers in the back."

On the day Mr. Sasaki came back to the shop we saw something unusual. For the first time I watched Teruo sell some old stuff to a customer. I heard the man plainly ask him if the flowers were fresh, and very clearly I heard Teruo reply, "Yes, sir. These flowers are fresh." I looked at Tommy and he winked back. When Teruo came to the back to make it into a bouquet, he looked as if he had a snail in his mouth. When Teruo went up front to complete the sale, Mr. Sasaki looked at Tommy and nodded approvingly.

When I went out to the truck to make my last delivery of the day Teruo followed me. "I feel rotten," he said to me. "Those flowers I sold to the people won't last longer than tomorrow. I feel lousy. I'm lousy. The people'll get to know my word is no good pretty soon."

"Forget it," I said. "Quit worrying. What's the matter with you?"

"I'm lousy," he said, and went back to the store.

Then early one morning it happened. While Teruo was selling the fresh flowers in the back to a customer, Mr. Sasaki came in quietly and watched the transaction. The boss didn't say anything at the time. All morning Teruo looked sick. He didn't know whether to explain to the boss or remain silent.

While Teruo was out to lunch Mr. Sasaki called us aside. "How long has this been going on?" he asked angrily.

"He's been doing it on and off. We told him to quit it," Tommy said. "He says he feels rotten selling old flowers."

"Old flowers!" snorted Mr. Sasaki. "I'll tell him plenty when he comes back. Old flowers! Maybe you can call them old at a roadside market, but they're not old in a flower shop."

"He feels guilty fooling the customers," Tommy explained.

The boss laughed impatiently. "That's no reason when you're in a business."

When Teruo came back he knew what was up. He looked at us for a moment and then went about cleaning the stems of the old flowers.

"Teruo," Mr. Sasaki called.

Teruo approached us as if readying himself for an attack.

"You've been selling fresh flowers and letting the old ones go to waste. I can't afford that, Teruo," Mr. Sasaki said. "Why don't you do as you're told? We all sell the flowers in the front. I tell you they're not old in a flower shop. Why can't you sell them?"

"I don't like it, Mr. Sasaki," Teruo said. "When the people ask me if they're fresh I hate to answer. I feel rotten after selling the old ones."

"Look here Teruo," Mr. Sasaki said, "I don't want to fire you. You're a good worker, and I know you need a job, but you've got to be a good clerk here or you're going out. Do you get me?"

"I get you," Teruo said.

The following morning we were all at the shop early. I had an eight o'clock delivery, and the others had to rush with a big order. Teruo was there already.

"Hello," he greeted us cheerfully as we came in.

He was unusually high-spirited, and I couldn't account for it. He was finishing up the eight o'clock delivery for me. He was almost through with it, adding some ferns, when Tommy came in.

When Mr. Sasaki arrived, Teruo waved his hand and cheerfully went about gathering some more flowers for another order. As he moved here and there it seemed as if he had forgotten that the three of us were in the shop. He looked at each vase, sizing up the flowers. He did this with great deliberation, as if he were the boss and had the last word in the shop. When a customer came in, Teruo swiftly waited on him as if he owned all the flowers in the world. When the man asked Teruo if he was getting fresh flowers, Teruo instantly escorted the customer into the rear and eventually sold him the fresh ones. He did it with so much grace, dignity and swiftness that we stood around feeling like his foolish assistants. However, Mr. Sasaki went on with his work as if nothing had happened.

Around noon Teruo waited on his second customer. He almost ran to greet an elderly lady who wanted an inexpensive bouquet for a dinner table. This time he not only went back to the rear for the fresh flowers, but added three or four extra ones. Tommy and I watched Mr. Sasaki fuming.

When the customer left the shop Mr. Sasaki came out of his office, furious. "You're a blockhead. You have no business sense. What are you doing here?" he said to Teruo. "Are you crazy?"

Teruo looked cheerful. "I'm not crazy, Mr. Sasaki," he said. "And I'm not dumb. I just like to do it that way, that's all."

The boss turned to Tommy and me. "That boy's a fool," he said.

Teruo laughed and walked off to the front with a broom. Mr. Sasaki shook his head. "What's the matter with him? I can't understand him," he said.

While the boss was out to lunch Teruo went on an amazing spree. He waited on three customers at one time, ignoring our presence. It was remarkable how he did it. He hurriedly took one customer's order and helped him write a card for it. He rushed to the second customer's side and persuaded her to buy some roses which were the freshest of the lot. She wanted them delivered so he jotted the address in the sales book. Then he hurried to the third customer.

"I want to buy that orchid in the window," she stated without hesitation.

"Do you have to have an orchid?" Teruo asked the lady.

"No," she said. "But I want something nice for tonight's dance, and I think the orchid will match my dress. Why do you ask?"

"If I were you I wouldn't buy that orchid," he told her. "It won't last. I could sell it to you and make a profit but I don't want to do that and spoil your evening. Come to the back, please, and I'll show you some of the nicest gardenias. They're fresh today."

We watched him pick out three of the biggest gardenias and make them into a corsage. When the lady went out with her package, a little boy came in and said he wanted to buy some flowers which didn't cost too much for his mother's birthday. Teruo waited on the boy. We saw him pick out a dozen expensive roses and give them to the kid.

Tommy nudged me. "If he were the boss he couldn't do those things," he said.

"In the first place," I said, "I don't think he could be a boss."

"What do you think?" Tommy said. "Is he crazy? Is he trying to get himself fired?"

"I don't know," I said.

When Mr. Sasaki returned, Teruo was waiting on a young lady.

"Did Teruo eat yet?" Mr. Sasaki asked Tommy.

"No, he won't go out. He says he's not hungry today," said Tommy.

We watched Teruo talking to the young lady. Then Teruo went to the rear and picked out a dozen of the very freshest white roses and brought them out to the lady.

"Aren't they lovely?" we heard her say.

We watched him come back, take down a box, place the roses neatly inside, and then give her the package. We watched him thank her, and we noticed her smile and say thanks. The lady walked out.

Mr. Sasaki ran excitedly to the front. "Teruo! She forgot to pay!"

Teruo stopped the boss from going out. "Wait, Mr. Sasaki," he said. "I *gave* them to her."

"What!" the boss cried indignantly.

"She came in just to look around and see the flowers. She likes pretty roses."

"What's the matter with you?" the boss said. "Are you crazy? What did she buy?"

"Nothing, I tell you," Teruo said. "I gave them to her because she admired them, and I liked her."

"You're fired! Get out!" Mr. Sasaki sputtered. "Don't come back to the store again."

"And I gave her fresh ones too," Teruo said.

Mr. Sasaki pulled out several bills from his wallet. "Here's your wages for this week. Now, get out," he said.

"I don't want it," Teruo said. "You keep it and buy some more flowers."

"Here, take it. Get out," Mr. Sasaki said.

Teruo took the bills. Then he rang up a sale on the cash register and placed the bills in the drawer.

"All right, I'll go now. I feel fine. I'm happy. Thanks to you." He waved his hand to Mr. Sasaki. "No hard feelings."

On the way out Teruo remembered us. He looked back. "Good-bye. Good luck," he said cheerfully to Tommy and me.

He walked out of the shop with his shoulders straight, head high, and whistling. He did not come back to see us again.

SELECTING DETAILS FROM THE STORY.
The following questions help you check your reading comprehension. Put an *x* in the box next to each correct answer.

1. When Teruo first started working at the Morning Glory Flower Shop, he
   - ☐ a. knew a great deal about the flower business.
   - ☐ b. knew nothing about the flower business.
   - ☐ c. was very familiar with the different kinds of gardening materials.

2. Selling old flowers to the customers made Teruo feel
   - ☐ a. happy.
   - ☐ b. clever.
   - ☐ c. lousy.

3. When a customer wanted to buy the orchid in the window, Teruo
   - ☐ a. advised her not to purchase it.
   - ☐ b. said she had made an excellent choice.
   - ☐ c. told her to speak to the boss.

4. Mr. Sasaki fired Teruo because the young man
   - ☐ a. was not willing to work hard.
   - ☐ b. insulted several customers.
   - ☐ c. gave away a dozen fresh roses.

KNOWING NEW VOCABULARY WORDS.
The following questions check your vocabulary skills. Put an *x* in the box next to each correct answer.

1. All the clerks in the shop eventually developed the technique of waiting on customers. The word *technique* means
   - ☐ a. problem.
   - ☐ b. reward.
   - ☐ c. method.

2. While Teruo was busy selling flowers to a customer, Mr. Sasaki came in and watched the transaction. Which phrase best defines the word *transaction*?
   - ☐ a. a business deal
   - ☐ b. lack of interest
   - ☐ c. passing of time

3. When Teruo sold a customer fresh flowers from the rear of the shop, Mr. Sasaki began fuming and calling Teruo a blockhead. As used here, the word *fuming* means
   - ☐ a. laughing.
   - ☐ b. explaining.
   - ☐ c. showing anger.

4. He looked closely at each vase, sizing up the flowers with great deliberation, as if he were the boss. What is the meaning of the word *deliberation*?
   - ☐ a. careful thought
   - ☐ b. little effort
   - ☐ c. great anger

	× 5 =	
NUMBER CORRECT		YOUR SCORE

	× 5 =	
NUMBER CORRECT		YOUR SCORE

IDENTIFYING STORY ELEMENTS. The following questions check your knowledge of story elements. Put an *x* in the box next to each correct answer.

1. "Say It with Flowers" is *set* in a
   - ☐ a. garden.
   - ☐ b. flower shop.
   - ☐ c. grocery store.

2. Which pair of words best *characterizes* Teruo?
   - ☐ a. industrious; honest
   - ☐ b. intelligent; lazy
   - ☐ c. greedy; polite

3. What happened first in the *plot* of the story?
   - ☐ a. Teruo waited on three customers at the same time.
   - ☐ b. Mr. Sasaki introduced Teruo to Tommy.
   - ☐ c. Teruo took the money Mr. Sasaki gave him and put it in the cash register.

4. In "Say It with Flowers," there is *conflict* over how
   - ☐ a. much to charge for the flowers.
   - ☐ b. early to open the shop.
   - ☐ c. truthful one should be with the customers.

LOOKING AT CLOZE. The following questions use the cloze technique to check your reading comprehension. Complete the paragraph by filling in each blank with one of the words listed below. Each word appears in the story. Since there are five words and four blanks, one of the words will not be used.

Orchids are among the most delicate and beautiful of flowers. Prized for their gorgeous colors and elegant shapes, they are, unfortunately, not _____ .
1
Most orchids are grown in greenhouses and are sold by _____ . However,
2
it is possible to grow orchids in your home if the _____ are properly
3
controlled. Whatever the time of year, most flower shops usually have a

_____ of orchids in stock.
4

conditions   inexpensive

impatiently

florists   display

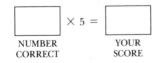

NUMBER
CORRECT

× 5 =

YOUR
SCORE

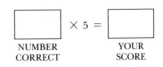

NUMBER
CORRECT

× 5 =

YOUR
SCORE

100

LEARNING HOW TO READ CRITICALLY. The following questions check your critical thinking skills. Put an *x* in the box next to each correct answer.

1. When he told a customer that some old flowers were fresh, Teruo "looked as if he had a snail in his mouth." This suggests that Teruo
   ☐ a. was very hungry.
   ☐ b. was quite pleased with himself.
   ☐ c. felt uncomfortable and ashamed.

2. Which of the following troubled Teruo?
   ☐ a. He believed that he wasn't making enough money.
   ☐ b. He was concerned that people would think that his word wasn't good.
   ☐ c. He was afraid he didn't know enough about the flower business.

3. Teruo probably put his wages in the cash register because
   ☐ a. Mr. Sasaki had already paid him.
   ☐ b. it wasn't worth his while to accept such a small sum.
   ☐ c. he wanted to pay Mr. Sasaki for the flowers he had given away.

4. Although Teruo had just been fired, he walked out of the shop "with his shoulders straight, head high, and whistling." This suggests that Teruo felt that he
   ☐ a. had been a failure as a clerk.
   ☐ b. had kept his self-respect.
   ☐ c. should never take any experience too seriously.

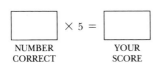

NUMBER
CORRECT

× 5 =

YOUR
SCORE

Improving Writing and Discussion Skills

- At the end of the story, Teruo told Mr. Sasaki, "I'm happy. Thanks to you." What was Teruo happy about? Why did he thank Mr. Sasaki? (Hint: think about Teruo's last day at the shop.)
- Mr. Sasaki explained that while the flowers might be considered old at a roadside market, they were not old in a flower shop. What did he mean by this? Do you agree with Mr. Sasaki's point of view? Why?
- A character in *Hamlet,* one of William Shakespeare's greatest plays, offers the following words of advice: "This above all: to thine own self be true." Show how this quotation applies to the story.

Use the boxes below to total your scores for the exercises. Then write your score on pages 140 and 141.

☐ **S**ELECTING DETAILS FROM THE STORY

+

☐ **K**NOWING NEW VOCABULARY WORDS

+

☐ **I**DENTIFYING STORY ELEMENTS

+

☐ **L**OOKING AT CLOZE

+

☐ **L**EARNING HOW TO READ CRITICALLY

▼

☐ **S**core Total: Story 11

12. The Empty Drum

by Leo Tolstoy

Meet the Author

Leo Tolstoy (1828–1910) is one of Russia's greatest novelists. Born near Moscow to wealthy parents, he spent a happy and carefree youth. As Tolstoy approached middle age, he became increasingly interested in social issues and the meaning of life. This resulted in his masterpieces, *War and Peace* and *Anna Karenina.* "The Empty Drum" is a good example of Tolstoy's concern with the values by which people live.

*E*milyan, who worked as a laborer, was crossing a meadow one day on his way to work, when he nearly stepped on a frog that hopped out right in front of him. He just managed to avoid it. Suddenly he heard someone calling from behind him. He looked around and saw a lovely girl, who said to him:

"Why don't you get married, Emilyan?"

"How can I marry?" said he. "I have nothing in this world but these clothes you see me in, and no one would have me for a husband."

"Well, then," said she, "take me for a wife."

Emilyan immediately fell in love with her. "I should like to," said he, "but where could we live?"

"Why worry about that?" said she. "All one has to do is work more and sleep less, and one can find food and clothing elsewhere."

"Very well then, let us be married," said he. "Where shall we go?"

"Let us go to the city."

So they went to the city and were married, and began living in a small cottage on the outskirts of the city.

103

One day the king, driving through the city, passed by Emilyan's cottage. Emilyan's wife came out to look at him. When the king saw her he was surprised. "Where did such a beauty come from?" he thought. He stopped his carriage, called Emilyan's wife and asked her, "Who are you?"

"The wife of Emilyan, the peasant," said she.

"Why did you, such a beautiful woman, marry a peasant? You ought to be the wife of a king."

"Thank you for your compliment," said she, "but I am very happy with my husband."

The king talked with her for a while and then rode on. He arrived at his palace, but he could not get Emilyan's wife out of his mind. He could not sleep all night, wondering how to get her away from Emilyan. He could think of no way of doing it, and therefore summoned his servants and told them to find a way.

The king's servants said, "Command Emilyan to come to the palace to work, and we will work him to death. His wife will be left a widow, and you will then be able to marry her."

The king followed the advice. He ordered Emilyan to work at the palace and to live at the palace with his wife.

The messengers came to Emilyan with the king's command. His wife said, "Go and work there during the day, but come back home at night."

Emilyan went, and when he reached the palace, the king's steward questioned him. "Why have you come alone, without your wife?"

"Why should I ask her to come here? She has a home."

At the palace they gave Emilyan more work

than two people could have completed, and he began without hope of finishing it. But lo and behold! When evening came it was all done. The steward saw that the job was finished and gave Emilyan four times as much work for the next day. Emilyan went home and found that the house had been swept, the oven was heated, the meal was ready, and that his wife was sitting by the table awaiting his return. She greeted him, set the table, served him supper, and then began to ask him about his work.

"Well," said he, "it's not so good. They gave me more work than I can do. They will kill me with work."

"Don't worry about your work," said she. "Don't look either behind you or ahead of you to see how much work you have done, or how much there is left to do. Just keep right on working, and all will be well."

So Emilyan went to sleep. The next morning he went to work again and toiled on without turning around even once. By evening it was all done, and as it grew dark he returned home for the night.

Again and again they kept increasing his tasks, but Emilyan always managed to complete them in time to go home for the night. After a week had passed this way, the king's servants saw that they could not wear Emilyan out by hard work and they began assigning him work that required skill. But this was also of no avail. No matter what they asked him to do—carpentry, masonry, or roofing—Emilyan completed it in time to go home to his wife at night. And a second week passed in this way.

Then the king summoned his servants and said, "Am I feeding you for nothing? Two weeks have passed and I fail to see what you have done. You were going to kill Emilyan with work, but from my window I can see him going home every evening—singing cheerfully! Are you trying to make fun of me?"

The servants began to make excuses. "We tried our very best to exhaust him," they said, "but he found nothing too difficult. No work—no matter how hard—seemed to tire him. Then we had him do things requiring skill, thinking he lacked the ability to do them—but he managed everything. Whatever task is put to him, he does it all. It's like magic! We have racked our brains trying to think of something he cannot do. We have finally decided to have him build a cathedral in just one day. Send for Emilyan and order him to build a cathedral opposite the palace in a single day. And if he does not succeed, let his head be cut off as punishment."

The king sent for Emilyan. "Listen well to my command," said he. "Build me a new cathedral on the square in front of my palace and have it completed by tomorrow evening. If it is ready I will reward you, but if you fail, your head will be cut off."

Emilyan heard the king's command, turned around, and went home. "Well," thought he, "the end is near for me." Arriving home he said, "Get ready, wife, we must flee from here at once, or I shall surely be lost."

"What has frightened you so?" she asked, "and why must we run away?"

"How can I not be frightened?" said he. "The king has ordered me to build a cathedral—in one day. If I fail he will have my head cut off. The only thing to do is fly from here while there is still time."

But his wife would not hear of this. "The king has many soldiers. They would catch us anywhere. We can't escape from him, so you must obey him as long as your strength holds out."

"But how can I obey him when the task is beyond my strength?"

"Listen, my dear, don't be worried. Eat your supper now and go to bed. Get up a little earlier tomorrow morning and everything will get done on time."

So Emilyan went to sleep. His wife awakened him the next morning.

"Go quickly," said she, "and build your cathedral. Here are nails and a hammer. There is still enough work there for the day."

Emilyan went to the city, and when he arrived at the palace square, there stood a large cathedral, almost finished. Emilyan started to work, and by evening he completed it.

The king looked out his window and saw the cathedral already built, with Emilyan driving in the last nails. And the king was not pleased to see the cathedral. He was angered not to be able to punish Emilyan and take away his wife. Again he called his servants. "Emilyan has finished his task, and there is no excuse for punishing him. Even this," he said, "was not too hard for him. A more clever plan must be devised—or I will punish you, as well as him."

So the king's servants suggested that he order Emilyan to make a river that would flow around the palace and have ships sailing on it. The king summoned Emilyan and explained his new task.

"Since," said he, "you were able to erect a cathedral in one day, you should be able to do this too. See to it that it is ready tomorrow, or else your head will be cut off."

Emilyan was even more downcast than before, and he returned, dejected, to his wife.

"Why are you so sad?" asked his wife. "Has the king given you some new task to perform?"

Emilyan told her about it. "We must fly," said he.

But his wife said, "There is no escaping the soldiers. They will catch us wherever we go. There is nothing to do but obey."

"But how can I obey?"

"Listen, my dear," said she, "don't be so gloomy. Eat your supper now and go to bed. Get up early, and all will be done in good time."

So Emilyan went to sleep. In the morning his wife awakened him.

"Go," said she, "to the palace. Everything is ready. At the wharf you will find one little mound of earth. Take your spade and level it. Then the task will be completed."

When Emilyan reached the city, he saw a river flowing around the palace, with ships sailing on it. When the king awoke he saw a river where there had not been one before. Ships were sailing up and down, and Emilyan was leveling a mound with a shovel. The king stared in awe, but neither the river nor the ships pleased him, so distressed was he at not being able to condemn Emilyan. "There is no task," thought he, "that he cannot manage. What is to be done?" And he called his servants and again asked their advice.

"Find some task," said he, "beyond Emilyan's power. For whatever you have demanded of him, he has thus far accomplished, and I cannot take his wife from him."

The king's servants pondered a long time, and at last they came to the king and said, "Send for Emilyan and say to him: 'Go somewhere, you don't know where, and bring back something, you don't know what.' Now there will be no escape for him, for wherever he goes, you can say he went to the wrong place, and whatever he brings back, you can say he brought back the wrong thing. Then you can order that he be killed and have his wife."

This pleased the king. "That," he said, "is a brilliant idea." And the king sent for Emilyan and said to him, "Go somewhere you don't know where, and bring back something you don't know what. If you fail, I will cut off your head."

Emilyan returned to his wife and told her what the king had said. His wife became thoughtful.

"This time," said she, "they have taught the king how to trap you. We must act wisely." She sat down and thought for a long time, and at last said to her husband: "You will have to go far away, to my grandmother, an old peasant woman, and you must ask for her help. She will give you something, and you must take it to the palace at once. I shall be there. I cannot escape them now. They will take me by force, but it will not be for long. If you listen to the old woman, you will quickly rescue me."

The wife prepared her husband for the journey. She gave him her spindle and said, "Give her this so that she will know you are my husband." And then she showed him the way to go.

Emilyan set off. He went beyond the city and came to a place where some soldiers were being drilled. Emilyan stopped to watch them. When the drill was over, the soldiers sat down to rest. Emilyan went up to them and asked, "Do you know the direction to 'somewhere I don't know where,' and where can I find 'something I don't know what'?"

The soldiers listened in amazement. "Who sent you on this errand?" they asked.

"The king," he replied.

"From the day we became soldiers, we have ourselves gone 'we don't know where,' and have sought, 'we don't know what.' We surely cannot help you."

After he had rested for a while, Emilyan continued on his way. He traveled on and on, and at last came to a forest where he saw a hut. In the hut sat a little old woman— the old peasant woman—spinning flax. When the old woman saw Emilyan, she yelled out to him, "What have you come here for?"

Emilyan gave her the spindle and said that his wife had sent it. The old woman nodded her head and began to question him. And Emilyan told her about his life: how he met and married the girl, how they had gone to live in the city, how he had toiled at the palace, how he had built the cathedral, and made a river with ships, and how the king had told him to go somewhere, he knew not where, and bring back something, he knew not what.

After the woman heard his story, she said to him, "All right, my son, sit down and have something to eat."

Emilyan ate, and the old woman told him, "Here is a ball of thread. Roll it in front of you, and follow it wherever it rolls. You will go far, till you get to the sea. There you will find a great city. Enter the city and ask for a night's lodging at the last house. There you will find what you are seeking."

"But how will I recognize it?"

"When you see that which men obey sooner than father or mother, that will be it. Seize it and take it to the king. If the king says it is not the right thing, answer him: 'If it is not the right thing, it must be smashed. Then beat the thing and take it down to the river, break it into pieces, and throw it into the water. Then you will get your wife back."

Emilyan said good-bye to the old woman and rolled the ball of thread in front of him. It rolled on and on until it reached the sea. By the sea stood a great city, and at the end of the city was a large house. There Emilyan asked for a night's lodging, and they took him in. He went to sleep, and was awakened early in the morning to hear a father calling his son and telling him to cut firewood. But the son would not obey. "It is too early," he said. "There's plenty of time." Then Emilyan heard the mother say, "Go, son, your father's bones ache. Would you have him do it himself? It is time to get up!"

"There's plenty of time," the son murmured and fell asleep again. He had just fallen asleep when there came from the street a loud noise that thundered and rattled. The son jumped up, quickly put on his clothes, and ran into the street. Emilyan jumped up, too, and followed him to see what a son obeys sooner than his father or mother. What he saw was a man walking along the street carrying a round thing which he beat with two sticks. And it was *this* which had made the thundering noise that the son had obeyed. Emilyan ran up closer, examined it, and saw that it was round like a small tub, with a skin stretched over both ends. He asked what it was called.

"A drum," he was told.

"And is it empty?"

"Yes, it is empty."

Emilyan was surprised. He asked the man to give him this thing, but he refused. So Emilyan didn't ask again and walked along, following the drummer. He walked after him the whole day, and when the drummer lay down to sleep, Emilyan seized the drum and ran off with it.

He ran and ran till at last he came back to his own city. He went to see his wife, but she was not at home. The day after he went away, they had taken her to the king. Emilyan went to the palace and told them to say to the king that "He, who went he knew not where, has returned, and brought back he knows not what."

When they told the king, he sent back word that Emilyan should return the next day.

But Emilyan insisted. "Tell the king I have come today, and have brought what he ordered me to bring. If he doesn't come out to me, I will go in to him."

The king came out. "Where have you been?" he asked.

"I don't know," Emilyan replied.

"What did you bring back?"

Emilyan pointed to the drum, but the king refused to look at it.

"That's not the right thing," he said.

"If it's not the right thing, it must be smashed," said Emilyan, "and good riddance to it!"

Emilyan left the palace and beat the drum. And as he did so, the king's army ran to follow him, saluting Emilyan and awaiting his commands.

From the window the king began to shout to his army, forbidding them to follow Emilyan. But they did not listen to what the king said and kept on following Emilyan.

When the king saw this, he ordered Emilyan's wife returned to him, and asked Emilyan to give him the drum.

"I cannot do that," said Emilyan. "I must smash it, and then throw the pieces into the river."

Emilyan went to the river, still carrying the drum, with the soldiers following him. At the bank of the river, Emilyan smashed the drum into pieces and threw them into the water. And the soldiers ran off in all directions. Then Emilyan took his wife and went home with her. From then on the king ceased to bother him, and they lived in happiness ever after.

SELECTING DETAILS FROM THE STORY.
The following questions help you check your
reading comprehension. Put an *x* in the box
next to each correct answer.

1. When the king saw Emilyan's wife he
   wondered
   - ☐ a. how old she was.
   - ☐ b. why he had never seen her before.
   - ☐ c. how such a beautiful woman had
     married a peasant.

2. The king ordered Emilyan to build a
   cathedral in
   - ☐ a. an hour.
   - ☐ b. a day.
   - ☐ c. a week.

3. Emilyan obtained the drum by
   - ☐ a. grabbing it from a boy who was
     marching in the street.
   - ☐ b. seizing it from a sleeping man.
   - ☐ c. buying it from a group of soldiers.

4. At the end of the story, Emilyan smashed
   the drum to pieces and threw the pieces
   - ☐ a. into the river.
   - ☐ b. at the king.
   - ☐ c. at the soldiers.

KNOWING NEW VOCABULARY WORDS. The
following questions check your vocabulary
skills. Put an *x* in the box next to each correct
answer.

1. The task seemed impossible to complete,
   so Emilyan became downcast and
   returned, dejected, to his wife. The word
   dejected means
   - ☐ a. encouraged.
   - ☐ b. discouraged.
   - ☐ c. entertained.

2. After the first plan failed, the king told
   his servants that a more clever plan must
   be devised. Which of the following best
   defines the word *devised*?
   - ☐ a. created
   - ☐ b. neglected
   - ☐ c. triumphed

3. They were married and lived in a small
   cottage on the outskirts of the city. What
   is the meaning of the word *outskirts*?
   - ☐ a. fog
   - ☐ b. edge
   - ☐ c. luxury

4. The king shouted angrily at his soldiers,
   forbidding them to follow Emilyan; the
   soldiers did not listen. As used here, the
   word *forbidding* means
   - ☐ a. destroying or wrecking.
   - ☐ b. leading or guiding.
   - ☐ c. prohibiting or not allowing.

	× 5 =	
NUMBER CORRECT		YOUR SCORE

	× 5 =	
NUMBER CORRECT		YOUR SCORE

IDENTIFYING STORY ELEMENTS. The following questions check your knowledge of story elements. Put an *x* in the box next to each correct answer.

1. Who is the *main character* in "The Empty Drum"?
   - ☐ a. Emilyan
   - ☐ b. Emilyan's wife
   - ☐ c. the king

2. What was the king's *motive* for wanting Emilyan killed?
   - ☐ a. The king was afraid that Emilyan would take over the army.
   - ☐ b. The king wanted to punish Emilyan for fooling his servants.
   - ☐ c. The king hoped to marry Emilyan's wife.

3. What happened last in the *plot* of "The Empty Drum"?
   - ☐ a. The old woman told Emilyan to follow a ball of thread wherever it rolled.
   - ☐ b. The king's servants suggested that Emilyan be worked to death.
   - ☐ c. The king ordered that Emilyan's wife be returned.

4. In this story there is *conflict* between
   - ☐ a. Emilyan and his wife.
   - ☐ b. Emilyan and the king.
   - ☐ c. the old woman and Emilyan.

LOOKING AT CLOZE. The following questions use the cloze technique to check your reading comprehension. Complete the paragraph by filling in each blank with one of the words listed below. Each word appears in the story. Since there are five words and four blanks, one of the words will not be used.

The _____ is thought to be the world's oldest musical instrument. In addition to producing music, the earliest drums also _____ as a method of communication. Drums were used to indicate the approach of an enemy, to signal a call to battle, or to _____ people together quickly. Because of the _____ tones produced by the drum, it was ideal for sounding an alarm.

thundering   served

condemn

drum   summon

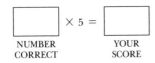

NUMBER CORRECT × 5 = YOUR SCORE

NUMBER CORRECT × 5 = YOUR SCORE

LEARNING HOW TO READ CRITICALLY.
The following questions check your critical
thinking skills. Put an *x* in the box next to
each correct answer.

1. Story clues indicate that Emilyan's wife
   ☐ a. had magical powers.
   ☐ b. was in love with the king.
   ☐ c. didn't care about what happened
        to Emilyan.

2. We may infer that Emilyan found his wife
   disguised as a frog and that he won her
   love through his
   ☐ a. strength.
   ☐ b. wealth.
   ☐ c. kindness.

3. Had the king commanded Emilyan to
   build an entire town, it is likely that
   Emilyan would have
   ☐ a. run away.
   ☐ b. succeeded at that task.
   ☐ c. failed at that task.

4. When Emilyan beat the drum, the soldiers
   saluted him, followed him, and awaited
   his commands. The author seems to be
   suggesting that
   ☐ a. the soldiers preferred Emilyan to
        the king.
   ☐ b. Emilyan would make an excellent
        general.
   ☐ c. soldiers will follow any leader.

Improving Writing and Discussion Skills

- When the king ordered Emilyan to
  "go somewhere you don't know where,
  and bring back something you don't
  know what," Emilyan's wife thought
  that task was the most troublesome
  so far. Why?
- In literature, a symbol is something
  that stands for something else. What
  do you think the empty drum stands
  for? What is meaningful about the
  fact that the drum is empty?
- At the time Tolstoy wrote "The Empty
  Drum," Russia was ruled by a czar
  who had all the power of a king.
  Suppose that the czar read the story.
  What do you believe he would think
  of it? Give reasons to support your
  opinion.

Use the boxes below to total your scores
for the exercises. Then write your score on
pages 140 and 141.

☐ SELECTING DETAILS FROM THE STORY
  +
☐ KNOWING NEW VOCABULARY WORDS
  +
☐ IDENTIFYING STORY ELEMENTS
  +
☐ LOOKING AT CLOZE
  +
☐ LEARNING HOW TO READ CRITICALLY
  ▼
☐ Score Total: Story 12

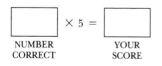

☐ × 5 = ☐

NUMBER   YOUR
CORRECT   SCORE

13. The Story of the Widow's Son

by Mary Lavin

This is the story of a widow's son, but it is a story that has two endings.

There was once a widow, living in a small neglected village at the foot of a steep hill. She had only one son, but he meant everything in life to her. She lived for his sake. She wore herself out working for him. Every day she made a hundred sacrifices in order to send him to a good school in a town four miles away, because there was a better teacher there than in the local village.

She made great plans for Packy, but she did not tell him about her plans. Instead, she threatened him day and night that if he didn't turn out well, she would put him to work on the roads or in the quarry under the hill.

But as the years went by, everyone in the village, and even Packy himself, could tell by the way she watched until he was out of sight in the morning, and watched until he came into sight in the evening, that he was

Meet the Author

Mary Lavin (1912–   ) was born in Massachusetts but moved to Ireland when she was nine years old. She has lived and worked there since. Lavin decided to become a writer after her first short story was published in *Dublin Magazine*. Although Lavin has written two highly praised novels, it is for her short stories that she has gained worldwide recognition. "The Story of the Widow's Son" is an excellent example of her storytelling art.

the beat of her heart, and that her gruff words were only to cover up her pride and joy in him.

It was for Packy's sake that she walked for hours along the road, letting her cow graze in the wild grass. It was for his sake she walked back and forth to the town to sell a few cabbages as soon as they were ripe. It was for his sake that she got up in the cold dawn hours to gather mushrooms for food and to sell. She bent her back daily to make every penny she could, and, as often happens, she made more by hard work out of her few sparse acres than many of the farmers around her made out of their great, lush meadows. Out of the money she made by selling eggs alone, she paid for Packy's clothes and his many books.

When Packy was in the graduating class in the school, the master had great hopes of his winning a scholarship to a big college in the city. He was getting to be a tall lad, and his character was strengthening, too, under his mother's sharp tongue. The people of the village were beginning to give him the same respect they gave to the sons of the well-to-do farmers who came home from their fine colleges in the summer with their expensive suits. And whenever they spoke to the widow, they praised him to the skies.

One day in June the widow was waiting at the gate for Packy. There had been no rain for some days and the hens and chickens were pecking irritably at the dry ground and wandering up and down the road in bewilderment. A neighbor passed by.

"Waiting for Packy?" said the neighbor, pleasantly, and he stood for a minute to take off his hat and wipe the sweat of the day from his face. He was an old man.

"It's a hot day!" he said. "It will be a hard ride for Packy on that battered old bike of his. I wouldn't like to have to travel four miles on a day like this!"

"Packy would travel three times that distance if there was a book at the end of the road!" said the widow, with the pride of those who cannot read more than a line or two without difficulty.

The minutes went by slowly. The widow kept looking up at the sun.

"I suppose the heat is better than the rain!" she said, at last.

"The heat can do a lot of harm too, though," said the neighbor, as he pulled a long blade of grass from between the stones of the wall and began to chew the end of it. "You could get sunstroke on a day like this!" He looked up at the sun. "The sun is a terror," he said. "It would cause you to drop down dead like a stone."

The widow looked up the hill in the direction of the town.

"He will have a good cool breeze coming down the hill, at any rate," she said.

The man looked up the hill.

"That's true. On the hottest day of the year you would get a cool breeze coming down that hill on a bicycle. And in the winter it's like knives peeling off your skin like you'd peel the bark off a branch." He chewed the grass thoughtfully. "That hill is a hill worthy of the name of a hill!" He took the grass out of his mouth. "It is my belief," he said earnestly, looking at the widow, "it is my belief that that hill has a name which can be found in the Ordnance Survey map!"

"If that's the case," said the widow, "Packy will be able to tell you all about it. When it isn't a book he's reading, it's a map."

"Is that so?" said the man. "That's interesting. A map is a great thing. It isn't everyone can properly read a map."

The widow wasn't listening.

"I think I see Packy!" she said, and she opened the wooden gate and stepped out into the roadway.

At the top of the hill there was a glitter of spokes as a bicycle came into sight. Then there was a flash of blue shirt as Packy came flying downward, gripping the handlebars of the bike, with his bright hair blowing back from his forehead. The hill was so steep, and he came down so fast, that it seemed to the man and woman at the bottom of the hill that he was not moving at all, but that it was the trees and bushes that were swiftly moving past him.

The hens and chickens clucked and squawked and ran along the road looking for a safe place. They ran to either side with fuss and chatter. Packy waved to his mother. He came nearer and nearer. They could see the freckles on his face.

"Shoo!" said Packy's mother, as she lifted her apron and flapped it in the air to frighten them out of his way.

It was only afterward, when the harm was done, that the widow began to think that it might, perhaps, have been the flapping of her own apron that scared the old clucking hen and sent it flying out over the garden wall into the middle of the road.

The old hen appeared suddenly and looked with a fearful eye at the hens and chickens as they ran to the right and the left. Her own feathers began to stand out from her. She craned her neck forward and gave a nervous squalk and fluttered about in the middle of the hot, dusty road.

Packy jammed on the brakes. The widow screamed. There was a flurry of white feathers and a spurt of blood. The bicycle swerved and fell. Packy was thrown over the handlebars.

It was such a simple accident that, although the widow screamed, and the old man looked around to see if help was near, neither of them thought that Packy was hurt very badly. But when they ran over and lifted his head, they saw that he could not speak. They wiped the blood from his face and looked around desperately, to measure the distance they would have to carry him.

It was only a few yards to the door of the cottage, but Packy was dead before they got him across the threshold.

"He's only in a weakness," screamed the widow, and she urged the crowd that gathered outside the door to do something for him. "Get a doctor," she cried, pushing a young laborer toward the door. "Hurry! Hurry! The doctor will bring him around."

The neighbors kept coming in the door from all sides. As soon as they saw the boy, stretched out flat on the bed, they knew that he was dead.

When at last the widow was convinced that her son was dead, the other women had to hold her down. She waved her arms and wrestled to get free. She wanted to wring the neck of every hen in the yard.

"I'll kill every one of them! What good are they to me now? All the hens in the world aren't worth one drop of human blood. That old clucking hen wasn't worth more than six shillings,[1] at the very most. What is six shillings? Is it worth poor Packy's life?"

But after a time she stopped raving and looked from one face to another.

"Why didn't he run over the hen?" she asked. "Why did he try to save an old hen

1. **shillings:** units of money.

that wasn't worth more than six shillings? Didn't he know he was worth more to his mother than an old hen that would be cooked in a pot one of these days? Why did he do it? Why did he put on the brakes going down one of the worst hills in the country? Why? Why?"

The neighbors patted her arm.

"There now!" they said. "There now!" And that was all they could think of saying, and they said it over and over again. "There now! There now!"

And years afterward, whenever the widow spoke of her son Packy to the neighbors who dropped in to keep her company for an hour or two, she always had the same question.

"Why did he put the price of an old hen above the price of his own life?"

And the people always gave her the same answer. "There now!" they said. "There now!" And they sat as silently as the widow herself, looking into the fire.

But surely some of those neighbors must have wondered what would have happened had Packy *not* yielded to his impulse and had, instead, ridden boldly over the old hen. And surely some of them must have stared into the flames of the fireplace and pictured the scene of the accident again, changing a detail here and there as they did so, and giving the story a different ending. For these people knew the widow, and they knew Packy, and when you know people well it is easy to guess what they will say and do in certain situations. So perhaps you will forgive me if I tell you what I myself think might have happened had Packy killed that old hen. And, in many ways, the new story is the same as the old one. It begins in the same way too.

There is the widow grazing her cow, and walking to town weighted down with sacks of cabbage that will pay for Packy's schooling. There she is, fussing over Packy in the mornings to make sure he is not late for school. There she is in the evening, watching the clock on the dresser for when he will appear on the top of the hill at his return. And there too, on a hot day in June, is the old man coming up the road, and pausing to talk to her as she stands at the door. There he is pulling a blade of grass from between the stones of the wall and putting it between his teeth to chew.

And when he opens his mouth at last it is to utter the same remark.

"Waiting for Packy?" said the old man, and then he took off his hat and wiped the sweat from his forehead. It will be remembered that he was an old man. "It's a hot day," he said.

"It's very hot," said the widow, looking anxiously up the hill.

"The heat is better than the rain, all the same," said the old man.

"I suppose it is," said the widow. "There were days when Packy came home drenched so bad that his clothes were stiff as boards."

"Is that so?" said the old man. "You may be sure he got a good hugging from you on those days. There is no son like a widow's son, eh? A little lamb!"

"Not Packy," said the widow in disgust. "Packy never got a day's hugging since the day he was born. I made up my mind from the start that I'd never make a soft one out of him."

The widow looked up the hill again.

"Here he is now!" she said, and they could see the glitter of the bicycle spokes and the flash of blue shirt as Packy came down the hill at a breakneck speed.

Nearer and nearer he came, faster and faster, waving his hand to the widow, shouting at the hens to leave the way!

The hens ran, stretching their necks in terror. Then unexpectedly, up from nowhere it seemed, came an old clucking hen. Packy stopped whistling. The widow screamed. Packy yelled and the widow flapped her apron. Then Packy swerved the bicycle, and a thick cloud of dust rose from the braked wheel.

It was difficult to see exactly what had happened. But Packy put his foot down and dragged it along the ground until he brought the bicycle to a stop. He threw the bicycle down on the hard road with a clatter and ran back. The widow could not bear to look. She threw her apron over her head.

"He's killed the hen!" she said. "He's killed her! He's killed her!" And then she let the apron fall back into place and began to run up the hill herself. The old man ran after the woman.

"Did you kill it?" screamed the widow. As she got near enough to see the blood and feathers, she raised her arm over her head. Her fist was clenched till the knuckles shone white. Packy cowered down and hunched up his shoulders as if to shield himself from a blow. His legs were splattered with blood, and the brown and white feathers of the dead hen were stuck to his hands and his clothes. Some of the feathers were still swirling with the dust in the air.

"I couldn't help it, Mother, I couldn't help it. I didn't see her until it was too late!"

The widow picked up the hen and examined it. Then, catching it by the leg, she raised it suddenly above her head and brought down the bleeding body on the boy's back, splattering the blood all over his face and hands, over his clothes, and over the dust of the road around him.

"How dare you lie to me!" she screamed, gasping. "You saw the hen, I know you saw it. You stopped whistling! You called out! We were watching you. We saw." She turned upon the old man. "Isn't that right?" she demanded. "He saw the hen, didn't he? He saw it?"

"It looked that way," said the old man, uncertainly.

"There you are!" said the widow. She threw the hen down on the road. "You saw the hen in front of you on the road, as plain as you see it now," she accused. "But you wouldn't stop to save it because you were in too big a hurry to get home to have your supper. Isn't that so?"

"No, Mother. No! I saw her all right but it was too late to do anything."

"He admits now that he saw it," said the widow, turning and nodding triumphantly at the onlookers who had gathered at the sound of the shouting.

"I never denied seeing it!" said the boy, appealing to the onlookers.

"He doesn't deny it," screamed the widow. "He stands there brazen as you like, and admits for all the world to hear that he saw the hen as plain as the nose on his face, and he rode over it without a thought!"

"But what else could I do?" said the boy, throwing out his hand, appealing to the crowd now, and appealing to the widow. "If I'd put on the brakes going down the hill at such a speed, I would have been thrown over the handlebars!"

"And what harm would that have done you?" screamed the widow. "I often saw you taking a tumble when you were wrestling with Jimmy Mack and I heard no complaints afterward, although your elbows and knees were scratched and your face was scraped." She turned to the crowd. "That's true I tell you." She swung back to Packy again. "You're not afraid of a fall when you go climbing trees, are you? You're not afraid to go up on the roof after a cat, are you? Oh, there's more in this than you want me to know. I can see that. You killed that hen on purpose—that's what I believe. You're tired of going to school. You want to get out of going away to college. That's it! You think if you kill the few poor hens we have, there will be no money saved when the time comes to pay for books and classes. That's it!"

Packy began to turn red.

"It's late in the day for me to be thinking of things like that," he said. "It's long ago I should have started those tricks if that was the way I felt. But it's not true. I want to go to college. The reason I was coming down the hill so fast was to tell you that I got the scholarship. The teacher told me just as I was leaving the schoolhouse. That's why I was pedaling so hard. That's why I was whistling. That's why I was waving my hand. Didn't you see me waving my hand once I came in sight at the top of the hill?"

The widow's hands fell to her sides. The wind of words died down within her and left her limp. She could feel the neighbors staring at her. She wished that they had gone away about their business. She wanted to throw out her arms to the boy and hug him like a small child. But she thought of how the crowd would look at each other and nod and snicker. A little lamb! She didn't want to satisfy them. If she gave into her feelings now, they would know how much she had been counting on his getting the scholarship. She wouldn't please them! She wouldn't satisfy them!

She looked at Packy, and when she saw him standing there before her, splattered with the feathers and blood of the dead hen, she felt a fierce resentment against him for killing the hen on this day of all days, and spoiling the great news of his success.

Her mind was confused. She stared at the blood on his face, and all at once it seemed as if the blood was a bad omen of his future. Fear, resentment, and defiance raised themselves within her like screeching animals. She looked from Packy to the onlookers.

"Scholarship! Scholarship!" she sneered. "I suppose you think you are a great fellow now? I suppose you think you can go off now, and look down on your poor slave of a mother who scraped and sweated for you with her cabbages and her hens? I suppose you think to yourself that it doesn't matter now whether the hens are alive or dead? Is that it, now? Well, let me tell you this! You're not as independent as you think. The scholarship may pay for your books and the teachers' fees, but who will pay for your clothes? Ah-ha, you forgot that, didn't you?" She put her hands on her hips.

Packy hung his head. He no longer appealed to the gawking neighbors. They might have been able to save him from blows, but he knew enough about life to know that no one could save him from shame.

The widow's heart burned at the sight of his shamed face, as her heart burned with grief, but her temper burned fiercer and fiercer, and she came to a point at which nothing could stop the blaze until it had burned itself out. "Who'll buy your suits?" she yelled. "Who'll buy your shoes?" She paused. What would embarrass and shame him the most? "Who'll buy your pajamas?"

she asked. "Or will you sleep in your skin?"

The neighbors laughed at that and the tension was broken. The widow herself laughed. She held her sides and laughed, and as she laughed everything seemed to take on a newer and simpler meaning. Things were not as bad as they seemed a moment before. She wanted Packy to laugh too. She looked at him. But as she looked at Packy, her heart turned cold with a strange new fear.

"Get into the house!" she said, giving him a push ahead of her. She wanted him safe under her own roof. She wanted to get him away from the gaping neighbors. She hated them, man, woman, and child. She felt that if they had not been there things would have been different. She wanted to mash a few potatoes and fry them up for Packy. That would comfort him. He loved that.

Packy hardly touched the food.

"Put on your good clothes," said the widow, making a great effort to be gentle. But her manner had become hard, and even the kindly offers she made sounded harsh. The boy sat slumped in the chair, which kept her nerves on edge and set up a conflict between the irritation and the love in her heart. She hated to see him slumping in the chair, but she was uneasy whenever he looked in the direction of the door. She felt safe while he was under her roof, under her eyes.

Next day she went to wake him up for school, but his room was empty. His bed had not been slept in, and when she ran out into the yard and called him everywhere, there was no answer. She ran up and down. She called at the houses of the neighbors, but he was not in any house. And she thought she could hear snickering behind her in each house that she left, as she ran to another. He wasn't in the village. He wasn't in the town. The master of the school said that she should let the police have a description of him. He said that he had never met a boy as sensitive as Packy. A boy like that took strange notions into his head from time to time.

The police did their best but there was no news of Packy that night. A few days later there was a letter saying that he was well. He asked his mother to notify the master that he would not be coming back, so that some other student could claim the scholarship. He said that he would send the price of the hen as soon as he made some money.

Another letter in a few weeks said that he had gotten a job on a ship, and that he would not be able to write very often, but that he would put aside some of his pay every week and send it to his mother whenever he got into port. He said that he wanted to pay her back for all she had done for him. He gave no address. He kept his promise about the money, but he never gave any return address when he wrote.

And so the villagers, sitting by the fireplace with the widow, may have let their thoughts run on this way. And this is what they may have pictured, as her complaining voice said the same thing over and over. "Why did he put the price of an old hen above the price of his own life?" And it is possible that their version of the story is just as true. For perhaps all our actions have the possibility of some other action. And sometimes the tragedy that fate hands us is better than the tragedy we bring upon ourselves.

SELECTING DETAILS FROM THE STORY.
The following questions help you check your
reading comprehension. Put an *x* in the box
next to each correct answer.

1. The widow made many sacrifices for Packy
   because she wanted him to
   ☐ a. go to a good school.
   ☐ b. wear expensive and stylish clothing.
   ☐ c. have plenty of cash to spend.

2. When Packy ran over the hen, his mother
   ☐ a. comforted him.
   ☐ b. screamed at him.
   ☐ c. praised him.

3. Packy explained that the reason he was
   coming down the road so fast was that
   ☐ a. the brakes on his bicycle failed.
   ☐ b. he was eager to tell his mother that
   he won the scholarship.
   ☐ c. he was very hungry and was
   hurrying home to have supper.

4. Packy sent his mother a letter in which
   he stated that he
   ☐ a. would return home in a few years.
   ☐ b. hoped she would write to him soon.
   ☐ c. would set aside some of every week's
   pay to send her.

KNOWING NEW VOCABULARY WORDS. The
following questions check your vocabulary
skills. Put an *x* in the box next to each correct
answer.

1. By working hard, the widow made more
   out of her few sparse acres than many
   of the farmers made out of their great,
   rich meadows. As used here, the word
   sparse means
   ☐ a. thin and poor.
   ☐ b. green and abundant.
   ☐ c. attractive and expensive.

2. "He doesn't deny it!" screamed the widow.
   "He stands there brazen as you like and
   admits . . . he rode over it without a
   thought!" Define the word *brazen*.
   ☐ a. shy
   ☐ b. bold
   ☐ c. uncertain

3. When the widow raised her arm, Packy
   cowered down and hunched up his
   shoulders as if to shield himself from a
   blow. The word *cowered* means
   ☐ a. drew back in fear.
   ☐ b. ran away at top speed.
   ☐ c. stood tall and straight.

4. The widow was filled with resentment
   at her son for killing the hen and spoiling
   the great news of the day. Someone who
   is filled with *resentment* feels
   ☐ a. frightened.
   ☐ b. pleased.
   ☐ c. angry.

	× 5 =	
NUMBER CORRECT		YOUR SCORE

	× 5 =	
NUMBER CORRECT		YOUR SCORE

IDENTIFYING STORY ELEMENTS. The following questions check your knowledge of story elements. Put an *x* in the box next to each correct answer.

1. Where is "The Story of the Widow's Son" *set*?
   - ☐ a. in a small village
   - ☐ b. in a large city
   - ☐ c. in the hustle and bustle of a busy town

2. Identify the statement that best *characterizes* the widow.
   - ☐ a. Although she was proud of her son, she did not think he was a good student.
   - ☐ b. Although she was proud of her son, her anger proved stronger than her pride.
   - ☐ c. Although she was proud of her son, she knew that none of her neighbors liked him.

3. Which of the following best describes the *mood* of the story?
   - ☐ a. strange and mysterious
   - ☐ b. light and amusing
   - ☐ c. sad and solemn

4. The most unusual thing about the *style* of "The Story of the Widow's Son" is that
   - ☐ a. it contains no dialogue.
   - ☐ b. there is no conflict between any of the characters.
   - ☐ c. it has two endings.

LOOKING AT CLOZE. The following questions use the cloze technique to check your reading comprehension. Complete the paragraph by filling in each blank with one of the words listed below. Each word appears in the story. Since there are five words and four blanks, one of the words will not be used.

In some places around the globe, the _____1_____ is the main means of transportation. Bicycles, of course, are far less _____2_____ to buy and operate than automobiles. In many cities, officials _____3_____ to the residents to use bicycles to travel to work because bicycles do not pollute the air. Moreover, it is _____4_____ to park about twenty bicycles in the space occupied by just one automobile.

impulse   possible

appeal

expensive   bicycle

	× 5 =	
NUMBER CORRECT		YOUR SCORE

	× 5 =	
NUMBER CORRECT		YOUR SCORE

LEARNING HOW TO READ CRITICALLY.
The following questions check your critical
thinking skills. Put an *x* in the box next to
each correct answer.

1. In both versions of the story
   ☐ a. Packy ran over the old hen.
   ☐ b. the boy died in an accident.
   ☐ c. the widow ended up losing her son.

2. For the widow, Packy "was the beat of her
   heart, and that her gruff words were only
   to cover up her pride and joy in him." This
   means that
   ☐ a. Packy meant a great deal to the
        widow—more than she admitted.
   ☐ b. Packy was often ill, which sometimes
        troubled the widow greatly.
   ☐ c. Packy knew of his mother's pride
        in him and sometimes took
        advantage of the situation.

3. We may infer that the reason Packy ran
   away was that
   ☐ a. he did not want to go to college.
   ☐ b. his mother shamed him so, he could
        no longer remain at home.
   ☐ c. he had always wanted to spend some
        time at sea.

4. Clues in the story suggest that the
   neighbors thought that the widow
   ☐ a. was wealthier than she appeared
        to be.
   ☐ b. acted calmly at all times.
   ☐ c. had a violent temper.

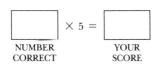

NUMBER   YOUR
CORRECT   SCORE

□ × 5 = □

Improving Writing and Discussion Skills

- Both versions of the story end in
  tragedy. Show how in each case the
  widow was responsible for what
  happened. In which version was she
  more responsible for what occurred?
  Explain your answer.
- The widow believed that "if the
  neighbors had not been there things
  would have been different." Do you
  agree? Why? When the widow looked
  at Packy at the end of the story, "her
  heart turned cold with a strange new
  fear." What was the fear the widow
  suddenly experienced? Explain.
- Suppose that there were a *third*
  version of the story—one in which
  Packy is injured. How do you think
  that story would end? Be creative.

Use the boxes below to total your scores
for the exercises. Then write your score on
pages 140 and 141.

☐ SELECTING DETAILS FROM THE STORY
+
☐ KNOWING NEW VOCABULARY WORDS
+
☐ IDENTIFYING STORY ELEMENTS
+
☐ LOOKING AT CLOZE
+
☐ LEARNING HOW TO READ CRITICALLY
▼
☐ Score Total: Story 13

14. Testimony of Trees

by Jesse Stuart

*W*e had just moved into the first farm we had ever owned when Jake Timmins walked down the path to the barn where Pa and I were nailing planks on a barn stall. Pa stood with a nail in one hand and his hatchet in the other while I stood holding the plank. We watched this small man with a thin face walk toward us. He took short steps and jabbed his sharpened cane into the ground as he hurried down the path.

"Wonder what he's after?" Pa asked as Jake Timmins came near the barn.

"Don't know," I said.

"Howdy, Mick," Jake said as he leaned on his cane and looked over the new barn that we had built.

"Howdy, Jake," Pa grunted. We had heard how Jake Timmins had taken men's farms. Pa was nervous when he spoke, for I watched the hatchet shake in his hand.

"I see ye're still putting improvements on yer barn," Jake said.

"Tryin' to get it fixed for winter," Pa told him.

Meet the Author

Jesse Stuart (1907–1984) is one of America's best-loved authors. He was born in a log cabin in the Kentucky hill country, an area that is the setting for many of his works. Stuart has written hundreds of short stories, numerous poems, and many articles and books. His popular autobiographical novel, *The Thread That Runs So True*, is an account of his experiences as a teacher in Kentucky and Ohio.

123

"I'd advise ye to stop now, Mick," he said. "Jist want to be fair with ye so ye won't go ahead and do a lot of work fer me fer nothing."

"How's that, Jake?" Pa asked.

"Ye've built yer barn on my land, Mick," he said with a little laugh.

"Ain't you joking, Jake?" Pa asked him.

"Nope, this is my land by rights," he told Pa as he looked our new barn over. "I hate to take this land with this fine barn on it, but it's mine and I'll have to take it."

"I'm afraid not, Jake," Pa said. "I've been around here since I was a boy. I know where the lines run. I know that ledge of rocks with that row of oak trees growing on it is the boundary line!"

"No it ain't, Mick," Jake said. "If it goes to court, ye'll find out. The boundary line runs from that big dead chestnut up there on the knoll, straight across this hollow to the top of the knoll up there where the twin hickory trees grow."

"But that takes my barn, my meadow, my garden," Pa said. "That takes ten acres of the best land I have. It almost gets my house!"

The hatchet quivered in Pa's hand and his lips trembled when he spoke.

"Tim Mennix sold ye land that belonged to me," Jake said.

"But you ought to have said something about it before I built my house and barn on it," Pa told Jake fast as the words would leave his mouth.

"Sorry, Mick," Jake said, "but I must be going. I've given ye fair warning that ye're building on my land!"

"But I bought this land," Pa told him. "I'm goin' to keep it."

"I can't help that," Jake told Pa as he turned to walk away. "Don't tear this barn down fer it's on my property!"

"Don't worry, Jake," Pa said. "I'm not tearing this barn down. I'll be feeding my cattle in it this winter!"

Jake Timmins walked slowly up the path the way he had come. Pa and I stood watching him as he stopped and looked our barn over; then he looked at our garden that we had fenced and he looked at the new house that we had built.

"I guess he'll be claiming the house too," Pa said.

And just as soon as Jake Timmins crossed the ledge of rocks that separated our farms, Pa threw his hatchet to the ground and hurried from the barn.

"Where are you going, Pa?" I asked.

"To see Tim Mennix."

"Can I go too?"

"Come along," he said.

We hurried over the mountain path toward Tim Mennix's shack. He lived two miles from us. Pa's shoes rustled the fallen leaves that covered the path. October wind moaned among the leafless treetops. Soon as we reached the shack we found Tim cutting wood near his woodshed.

"What's the hurry, Mick?" Tim asked Pa who stood wiping sweat from his October-leaf-colored face with his blue bandanna.

"Jake Timmins is tryin' to take my land," Pa told Tim.

"Ye don't mean it?"

"I do mean it," Pa said. "He's just been to see me and he said the land where my barn, garden, and meadow were belonged to him. Claims about ten acres of the best land I got. I told him I bought it from you and he said it didn't belong to you to sell."

"That ledge of rocks and the big oak trees

124

that grow along the backbone of the ledge has been the boundary line fer seventy years," Tim said. "But lissen, Mick, when Jake Timmins wants a piece of land, he takes it."

"People told me he's like that," Pa said. "I was warned against buying my farm because he's like that. People said he'd steal all my land if I lived next to him ten years."

"He'll have it before then, Mick," Tim Mennix told Pa in a trembling voice. "He didn't have but an acre to start from. That acre was a bluff where three farms joined and no one fenced it in because it was worthless and they didn't want it. He had a deed made fer this acre and he's had forty lawsuits when he set his fence over on other people's farms and took their land. But he goes to court and wins every time."

"I'll have the County Surveyor, Finn Madden, to survey my lines," Pa said.

"That won't help any," Tim told Pa. "There's been more people killed over the lines that he's surveyed than has been killed over any other one thing in this county. Surveyor Finn Madden's a good friend to Jake."

"But he's the County Surveyor," Pa said. "I'll have to have him."

"Jake Timmins is a dangerous man," Tim Mennix warned Pa. "He's dangerous as a loaded double-barrel shotgun."

"I've heard that," Pa said. "I don't want any trouble. I'm a married man with a family."

When we reached home, we saw Jake upon the knoll at the big chestnut tree sighting across the hollow to the twin hickories on the knoll above our house. And as he sighted across the hollow, he walked along and drove stakes into the ground. He set one stake in our front yard, about five feet from the corner of our house. Pa started out on him once but Mom wouldn't let him go. Mom said let the law settle the dispute over the land.

And that night Pa couldn't go to sleep. I was awake and heard him walking the floor when the clock struck twelve. I knew that Pa was worried, for Jake was the most feared man among our hills. He had started with one acre and now had over four hundred acres that he had taken from other people.

Next day Surveyor Finn Madden and Jake ran a boundary line across the hollow just about on the same line that Jake had surveyed with his own eyes. And while Surveyor Finn Madden looked through the instrument, he had Jake set the stakes and drive them into the ground with an ax. They worked at the line all day. And when they had finished surveying the line, Pa went up on the knoll at the twin hickories behind our house and asked Surveyor Finn Madden if his line was right.

"Surveyed it right with the deed," he told Pa. "Tim Mennix sold you land that didn't belong to him."

"Looks like this line would've been surveyed before I built my barn," Pa said.

"Can see why it wasn't," he told Pa. "Looks like you're losing the best part of your farm, Mick."

Then Surveyor Finn Madden, a tall man with a white beard, and Jake Timmins went down the hill together.

"I'm not so sure that I'm losing the best part of my farm," Pa said. "I'm not goin' to sit down and take it! I know Jake's a land thief and it's time his stealing land is stopped."

"What are you goin' to do, Pa?" I asked.

"Don't know," he said.

"You're not goin' to hurt Jake over the land, are you?"

He didn't say anything but he looked at the two men as they turned over the ledge of rocks and out of sight.

"You know Mom said the land wasn't worth hurting anybody over," I said.

"But it's my land," Pa said.

And that night Pa walked the floor. And Mom got out of bed and talked to him and made him go to bed. And that day Sheriff Eif Whiteapple served a notice on Pa to keep his cattle out of the barn that we had built. The notice said that the barn belonged to Jake Timmins. Jake ordered us to put our chickens up, to keep them off his garden when it was our garden. He told us not to let anything trespass on his land and his land was on the other side of the stakes. We couldn't even walk in part of our yard.

"He'll have the house next if we don't do something about it," Pa said.

Pa walked around our house in deep thought. He was trying to think of something to do about it. Mom talked to him. She told him to get a lawyer and fight the case in court. But Pa said something had to be done to prove that the land belonged to us, though we had a deed for our land in our trunk. And before Sunday came, Pa dressed in his best clothes.

"Where're you a-going, Mick?" Mom asked.

"To see Uncle Mel," he said. "He's been in a lot of boundary line-fence fights and he could give me some good advice!"

"We hate to stay here and have you gone, Mick," Mom said.

"Just don't step on property Jake laid claim to until I get back," Pa said. "I'll be back soon as I can. Some time next week you can look for me."

Pa went to West Virginia to get Uncle Mel. And while he was gone, Jake Timmins hauled wagonloads of hay and corn to the barn that we had built. He had taken over as if it were his own and as if he would always have it. We didn't step beyond the stakes where Surveyor Finn Madden had surveyed. We waited for Pa to come. And when Pa came, Uncle Mel came with him carrying a long-handled ax. Before they reached the house, Pa showed Uncle Mel the land Jake Timmins had taken.

"Land hogs are poison as copperhead snakes," Uncle Mel said. Uncle Mel was eighty-two years old, but his eyes were keen and his shoulders were broad and his hands were big and rough. He had been a timber cutter all his days and he was still cuttin' timber in West Virginia at the age of eighty-two. "He can't do this to ye, Mick!"

Uncle Mel was madder than Pa when he looked over the new line that they had surveyed from the dead chestnut on one knoll to the twin hickory trees on the other knoll.

"Anybody would know the boundary line wouldn't go like that," Uncle Mel said. "The line would follow the ridge."

"Looks that way to me too," Pa said.

"He's stealin' yer land, Mick," Uncle Mel said. "I'll help ye get yer land back. He'll never beat me. I've had to fight too many squatters tryin' to take my land. I know how to fight 'em with the law."

That night Pa and Uncle Mel sat before the fire and Uncle Mel looked over Pa's deed. Uncle Mel couldn't read very well and when he came to a word he couldn't read, I told him what it was.

"We'll have to have a court order first, Mick," Uncle Mel said. "When we get the court order, I'll find the line."

I didn't know what Uncle Mel wanted with

a court order, but I found out after he got it. He couldn't chop on a tree on the boundary line until he got an order from the court. And soon as Pa got the court order and gathered a group of men for witnesses, Uncle Mel started work on the line fence.

"Sixteen rods from the dead chestnut tree due north," Uncle Mel said, and we started measuring sixteen rods due north.

"That's the oak tree, there," Uncle Mel said. It measured exactly sixteen rods from the dead chestnut to the black oak tree.

"The deed said the oak was blazed,"[1] Uncle Mel said, for he'd gone over the deed until he'd memorized it.

"See the scar, men," Uncle Mel said.

"But that was done seventy years ago," Pa said.

"Funny about the testimony of trees," Uncle Mel told Pa, Tim Mennix, Orbie Dorton, and Dave Sperry. "The scar will always stay on the outside of a tree well as on the inside. The silent trees will keep their secrets."

Uncle Mel started chopping into the tree. He swung his ax over his shoulder and bit out a slice of wood every time he struck. He cut a neat block into the tree until he found a dark place deep inside the tree.

"Come, men, and look," Uncle Mel said. "Look at that scar. It's as pretty a scar as I ever seen in the heart of a tree!"

And while Uncle Mel wiped sweat with his blue bandanna from his white beard, we looked at the scar.

"It's a scar, all right," Tim Mennix said, since he had been a timber cutter most of his life and knew a scar on a tree.

"Think that was cut seventy years ago?"

Orbie Dorton said. "That's when the deed was made and the old survey was run."

"We'll see if it's been seventy years ago," Uncle Mel said as he started counting the rings in the tree. "Each ring is a year's growth."

We watched Uncle Mel pull his knife from his pocket, open the blade, and touch each ring with his knife-blade point as he counted the rings across the square he had chopped into the tree. Uncle Mel counted exactly seventy rings from the bark to the scar.

"Ain't it the boundary line tree, boys?" Uncle Mel asked.

"Can't be anything else," Dave Sperry said.

And then Uncle Mel read the deed, which called for a mulberry tree thirteen rods due north from the black oak. We measured to the mulberry and Uncle Mel cut his notch to the scar and counted the rings. It was seventy rings from the bark to the scar. Ten more rods we came to the poplar the deed called for, and he found the scar on the outer bark and inside the tree. We found every tree the deed called for but one, and we found its stump. We surveyed the land from the dead chestnut to the twin hickories. We followed it around the ledge.

"We have the evidence to take to court," Uncle Mel said. "I'd like to bring the jury right here to this line fence to show 'em."

"I'll go right to town and put this thing in court," Pa said.

"I'll go around and see the men that have lost land to Jake Timmins," Uncle Mel said. "I want 'em to be at the trial."

Before our case got to court, Uncle Mel had shown seven of our neighbors how to trace their boundary lines and get their land back from Jake Timmins. And when our trial was called, the courthouse was filled with

---

1. **blazed:** marked by cutting off a piece of bark to indicate a boundary.

people who had lost land and who had disputes with their neighbors over line fences, attending the trial to see if we won. Jake Timmins, Surveyor Finn Madden, and their lawyer, Henson Stapleton, had produced their side of the question before the jurors and we had lawyer Sherman Stone and our witnesses to present our side, while all the landowners Jake Timmins had stolen land from listened to the trial. The foreman of the jury asked that the members of the jury be taken to the line fence.

"Now here's the way to tell where a line was blazed on saplings seventy years ago," Uncle Mel said, as he showed them the inner mark on the line oak; then he showed them the outward scar. Uncle Mel took them along the boundary line and showed them each tree that the deed called for, all but the one that had fallen.

"It's plain as the nose on your face," Uncle Mel would say every time he explained each line tree. "There's too many land thieves in this county and a county surveyor who's the worst liar in the bunch."

After Uncle Mel had explained the line fence to the jurors, they followed Sheriff Whiteapple and his deputies back to the courtroom. Pa went with them to get the decision. Uncle Mel waited at our house for Pa to return.

"That land will belong to Mick," Uncle Mel told us. "And the hay and corn in that barn will belong to him."

When Pa came home, there was a smile on his face.

"It's yer land, ain't it, Mick?" Uncle Mel asked.

"It's still my land," Pa said, "and sixteen men are now filing suits to recover their land. Jake Timmins won't have but an acre left."

"Remember the hay and corn he put in yer barn is yours," Uncle Mel said.

Uncle Mel got up from his chair, stretched his arms. Then he said, "I must be back on my way to West Virginia."

"Can't you stay longer with us, Uncle Mel?" Pa said.

"I must be gettin' back to cut timber," he said. "If ye have any more land troubles, write me."

We tried to get Uncle Mel to stay longer. But he wouldn't stay. He left with his long-handled ax across his shoulder. We waved good-by to him as he walked slowly down the path and out of sight on his way to West Virginia.

SELECTING DETAILS FROM THE STORY.
The following questions help you check your
reading comprehension. Put an *x* in the box
next to each correct answer.

1. Jake Timmins was known for
   - ☐ a. building barns.
   - ☐ b. cutting timber.
   - ☐ c. stealing land.

2. Uncle Mel needed a court order so that
   he could
   - ☐ a. cut down the trees on the boundary line.
   - ☐ b. chop into the trees on the boundary line.
   - ☐ c. measure the trees on the boundary line.

3. To determine if the scar on the tree
   had been made seventy years before,
   Uncle Mel
   - ☐ a. counted the rings from the bark to the scar.
   - ☐ b. spoke to people who lived in the area many years before.
   - ☐ c. went over the deed until he memorized it.

4. At the end of the story Mick not only
   recovered his land but also
   - ☐ a. received a cash settlement from Jake.
   - ☐ b. was entitled to the hay and corn that Jake put into the barn.
   - ☐ c. got an apology from Finn Madden, the county surveyor.

KNOWING NEW VOCABULARY WORDS. The
following questions check your vocabulary
skills. Put an *x* in the box next to each correct
answer.

1. Pa wiped sweat from his face with his blue
   bandanna. A *bandanna* is a
   - ☐ a. pair of gloves.
   - ☐ b. bag for leaves.
   - ☐ c. large handkerchief.

2. Mom said not to fight Jake Timmins over
   the land but to let the law settle the
   dispute. As used here, the word *dispute*
   means
   - ☐ a. quarrel.
   - ☐ b. agreement.
   - ☐ c. danger.

3. The scar on the inside of the tree offered
   testimony about when the boundary line
   had been made. The word *testimony* means
   - ☐ a. an interesting question.
   - ☐ b. proof or evidence.
   - ☐ c. an unusual disease.

4. Jake said the meadow and garden
   belonged to him, to keep the chickens
   away, and not let anyone trespass on his
   land. When you *trespass,* you
   - ☐ a. go on someone's property without permission.
   - ☐ b. argue about where to build a fence.
   - ☐ c. plant trees in a straight line.

☐ × 5 = ☐
NUMBER   YOUR
CORRECT   SCORE

☐ × 5 = ☐
NUMBER   YOUR
CORRECT   SCORE

IDENTIFYING STORY ELEMENTS. The following questions check your knowledge of story elements. Put an *x* in the box next to each correct answer.

1. Which statement best *characterizes* Jake Timmins?
   ☐ a. He was tall with keen eyes, broad shoulders, and a white beard.
   ☐ b. He was small, walked with a cane, and was feared by his neighbors.
   ☐ c. He was cheerful and friendly.

2. What happened last in the *plot* of "Testimony of Trees"?
   ☐ a. Uncle Mel showed the trees along the boundary line to the members of the jury.
   ☐ b. The sheriff served a notice on Mick to keep off Jake Timmins's land.
   ☐ c. Jake advised Mick not to make any improvements on the barn.

3. "The scar will always stay on the outside of a tree well as on the inside." This line of *dialogue* was spoken by
   ☐ a. Finn Madden.
   ☐ b. Jake Timmins.
   ☐ c. Uncle Mel.

4. The *climax* of the story occurred when
   ☐ a. Uncle Mel said he'd help Mick recover his land.
   ☐ b. Jake bought an acre of land where three farms joined.
   ☐ c. Finn Madden surveyed the boundary line.

	× 5 =	
NUMBER CORRECT		YOUR SCORE

LOOKING AT CLOZE. The following questions use the cloze technique to check your reading comprehension. Complete the paragraph by filling in each blank with one of the words listed below. Each word appears in the story. Since there are five words and four blanks, one of the words will not be used.

Redwoods are among the tallest

_____ in the world. While most
            1

redwoods grow to a height of 200–300 feet,

one redwood has been _____
                                    2

at a record 385 feet. The trunk of the

redwood is generally 8–12 feet in diameter,

with _____ that can be as much
          3

as 12 inches thick. Forests of this magnificent

tree _____ from southern
              4

Oregon to central California along the West

Coast of the United States.

witnesses   bark

stretch

measured   trees

	× 5 =	
NUMBER CORRECT		YOUR SCORE

130

LEARNING HOW TO READ CRITICALLY.
The following questions check your critical
thinking skills. Put an *x* in the box next to
each correct answer.

1. We may infer that as a result of what
   happened in the story,
   □ a. Jake Timmins and Mick will
         eventually become good friends.
   □ b. Jake will eventually lose all the land
         suits brought against him.
   □ c. Uncle Mel will eventually send Mick
         a bill for his services.

2. Evidence in the story indicates that
   Jake Timmins and Finn Madden
   □ a. simply made some honest mistakes.
   □ b. were working together to steal land
         from people.
   □ c. were highly respected by the people
         who lived in the county.

3. If there are fifty rings in a tree, we may
   conclude that the tree
   □ a. is the tallest one in the area.
   □ b. must have been hit by lightning.
   □ c. is fifty years old.

4. The story suggests that if a person is
   attempting to cheat you, the appropriate
   way to handle the situation is to
   □ a. get the proper evidence and then
         resolve the matter in a court of law.
   □ b. threaten to kill the individual who
         is trying to cheat you.
   □ c. think of some vicious ways to get
         even with that person.

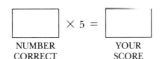

NUMBER   YOUR
CORRECT   SCORE

Improving Writing and Discussion Skills

- Why is the selection called
  "Testimony of Trees"? Think of
  another interesting and appropriate
  title for the story.
- The author indicates that Finn
  Madden was "a good friend to Jake."
  Why is this important for the reader
  to know? Why do you think Jake won
  all the previous land cases brought
  against him? Following Mick's
  winning suit against Jake, what do
  you think the county will do about
  surveyor Finn Madden?
- Suppose you were a reporter assigned
  to cover the trial for a local newspaper. Write the news story, including
  as many facts as possible. If you wish,
  make up a headline for your story.

Use the boxes below to total your scores
for the exercises. Then write your score on
pages 140 and 141.

☐   **S**ELECTING DETAILS FROM THE STORY
 +

☐   **K**NOWING NEW VOCABULARY WORDS
 +

☐   **I**DENTIFYING STORY ELEMENTS
 +

☐   **L**OOKING AT CLOZE
 +

☐   **L**EARNING HOW TO READ CRITICALLY
 ▼

☐   **S**core Total: Story 14

15. You Can't Take It with You

by Eva-Lis Wuorio

*T*here was no denying two facts. Uncle Basil was rich. Uncle Basil was a miser.

The family were unanimous about that. Gentle Aunt Clotilda, who wanted a new string of pearls because the one she had was getting old, had merely called him *Scrooge* Basil. Percival, having again smashed his Aston Martin,[1] for which he had not paid, had declared Uncle Basil a skinflint, miser, tightwad, with colorful adjectives added.

"He doesn't have to be parsimonious,[2] that's true, with all he has," said Percival's mother. "But you shouldn't use rude words, Percival. They might get back to him."

"He can't take it with him," said Percival's sister Letitia, combing her golden hair. "I need a new fur but he said, 'Why? It's summer.' Well! He's mingy,[3] that's what he is."

---

1. **Aston Martin:** an expensive English sports car.
2. **parsimonious:** very stingy; miserly.
3. **mingy:** a combination of mean and stingy.

Meet the Author

Eva-Lis Wuorio (1918–   ) was born in Finland but later moved to Canada where she worked as an editor and journalist. She has written many children's books including the award-winning *The Island of Fish in the Trees.* One of her most popular novels is *To Fight in Silence,* set in Norway and Denmark during World War II. "You Can't Take It with You" appears in *Escape If You Can,* a collection of thirteen unusual tales.

"He can't take it with him" was a phrase the family used so often it began to slip out in front of Uncle Basil as well.

"You can't take it with you, Uncle Basil," they said. "Why don't you buy a sensible house out in the country, and we could all come and visit you? Horses. A swimming pool. The lot. Think what fun you'd have, and you can certainly afford it. You can't take it with you, you know."

Uncle Basil had heard all the words they called him because he wasn't as deaf as he made out. He knew he was a mingy, stingy, penny-pinching hoarder, and curmudgeon[4] (just to start with). There were other words, less gentle, he'd also heard himself called. He didn't mind. What galled him was the often-repeated warning, "You can't take it with you." After all, it was all his.

He'd gone to the Transvaal[5] when there was still gold to be found if one knew where to look. He'd found it. They said he'd come back too old to enjoy his fortune. What did they know? He enjoyed simply having a fortune. He enjoyed also saying no to them all. They were like circus animals, he often thought, behind the bars of their demands of something for nothing.

Only once had he said yes. That was when his sister asked him to take on Verner, her somewhat slow-witted eldest son. "He'll do as your secretary," his sister Maud had said. Verner didn't do at all as a secretary, but since all he wanted to be happy was to be told what to do, Uncle Basil let him stick around as an all-around handyman.

Uncle Basil lived neatly in a house very much too small for his money, the family said,

in an unfashionable suburb. It was precisely like the house where he had been born. Verner looked after the small garden, fetched the papers, and filed his nails when he had time. He had nice nails. He never said to Uncle Basil, "You can't take it with you," because it didn't occur to him.

Uncle Basil also used Verner to run messages to the bank, and such, since he didn't believe either in the mails or the telephone. Verner got used to carrying thick envelopes back and forth without ever bothering to question what was in them. Uncle Basil's lawyers, accountants, and bank managers also got used to his business methods. He did have a fortune, and he kept making money with his investments. Rich men have always been allowed their foibles.

Another foible of Uncle Basil's was that, while he still was in excellent health, he had Verner drive him out to an old-fashioned carpenter shop, where he had himself measured for a coffin. He wanted it roomy, he said.

The master carpenter was a countryman of the same generation as Uncle Basil, and he accepted the order matter-of-factly. They consulted about woods and prices, and settled on a medium-price, unlined coffin. A lined one would have cost double.

"I'll line it myself," Uncle Basil said. "Or Verner can. There's plenty of time. I don't intend to pop off tomorrow. It would give the family too much satisfaction. I like enjoying my fortune."

Then one morning, while in good humor and sound mind, he sent Verner for his lawyer. The family got to hear about this, and there were fights and general quarreling while they tried to find out to whom Uncle Basil had decided to leave his money. To put them out

4. **curmudgeon:** a very bad-tempered, difficult person.
5. **Transvaal:** a province of the Republic of South Africa.

of their misery, he said, he'd tell them the truth. He didn't like scattering money about. He liked it in a lump sum. Quit bothering him about it.

That happened a good decade before the morning his housekeeper, taking him his tea, found him peacefully asleep forever. It had been a good decade for him. The family hadn't dared to worry him, and his investments had risen steadily.

Percival, always pressed[6] for money, had threatened to put arsenic in his tea, but when the usual proceedings were gone through, Uncle Basil was found to have died a natural death. "A happy death," said the family. "He hadn't suffered."

They began to remember loudly how nice they'd been to him and argued about who had been the nicest. It was true too. They had been attentive, the way families tend to be to rich and stubborn elderly relatives. They didn't know he'd heard all they'd said out of his hearing, as well as the flattering drivel they'd spread like soft butter on hot toast in his hearing. Everyone, recalling his own efforts to be thoroughly nice, was certain that he and only he would be the heir to the Lump Sum.

They rushed to consult the lawyer. He said that he had been instructed by Uncle Basil in precise terms. The cremation was to take place immediately after the death, and they would find the coffin ready in the garden shed. Verner would know where it was.

"Nothing else?"

"Well," said the lawyer in the way lawyers have, "he left instructions for a funeral repast to be sent in. Everything of the best. Goose and turkey, venison and beef, oysters and lobsters. He liked a good send-off, curmudgeon though he was, he'd said."

The family was a little shaken by the use of the word "curmudgeon." How did Uncle Basil know about that? But they were relieved to hear that the lawyer also had an envelope, the contents of which he did not know, to read to them at the feast after the cremation.

They all bought expensive black clothes, since black was the color of that season anyway, and whoever inherited would share the wealth. That was only fair.

Only Verner said couldn't they buy Uncle Basil a smarter coffin? The one in the garden shed was pretty tatty, since the roof leaked. But the family hardly listened to him. After all, it would only be burned, so what did it matter?

So, duly and with proper sorrow, Uncle Basil was cremated.

The family returned to the little house as the housekeeper was leaving. Uncle Basil had given her a generous amount of cash, telling her how to place it so as to have a fair income for life. In gratitude she spread out the goodies, but she wasn't prepared to stay to do the dishes.

They were a little surprised, but not dismayed, to hear from Verner that the house was now in his name. Uncle Basil had also given him a small sum of cash and told him how to invest it. The family taxed[7] him about it, but the amount was so nominal[8] they were relieved to know Verner would be off their hands. Verner himself, though mildly missing the old man because he was used to him, was quite content with his lot. He wasn't used

6. **pressed:** troubled.

7. **taxed:** criticized or blamed.
8. **nominal:** very small.

134

to much, so he didn't need much.

The storm broke when the lawyer finally opened the envelope.

There was only one line in Uncle Basil's scrawl.

"I did take it with me."

Of course there was a great to-do. What about the fortune? The millions and millions!

Yes, said the accountants, and even the bank managers, who finally admitted, yes, there had been a very considerable fortune. Uncle Basil, however, had drawn large sums in cash, steadily and regularly, over the past decade. What had he done with it? That the accountants and the bank managers did

not know. After all, it had been Uncle Basil's money, his affair.

Not a trace of the vast fortune ever came to light.

No one thought to ask Verner, and it didn't occur to Verner to volunteer that for quite a long time he had been lining the coffin, at Uncle Basil's behest, with thick envelopes he brought back from the bank. First he'd done a thick layer of these envelopes all around the sides and bottom of the coffin. Then, as Uncle Basil wanted, he'd tacked on blue cloth.

He might not be so bright in his head but he was smart with his hands.

He'd done a neat job.

SELECTING DETAILS FROM THE STORY.
The following questions help you check your
reading comprehension. Put an *x* in the box
next to each correct answer.

1. The family tried to convince Uncle Basil to
   - ☐ a. invest his money wisely.
   - ☐ b. keep his fortune in the bank.
   - ☐ c. buy a house in the country.

2. Verner worked for Uncle Basil as
   - ☐ a. a lawyer.
   - ☐ b. a master carpenter.
   - ☐ c. an all-around handyman.

3. Uncle Basil decided to buy a coffin that was
   - ☐ a. very expensive.
   - ☐ b. medium-priced and unlined.
   - ☐ c. as small as possible.

4. At the end of the story, Uncle Basil's vast fortune was
   - ☐ a. never found.
   - ☐ b. shared by the family.
   - ☐ c. given to Verner.

KNOWING NEW VOCABULARY WORDS. The
following questions check your vocabulary
skills. Put an *x* in the box next to each correct
answer.

1. Uncle Basil didn't mind when his family called him a miser, but it galled him when they said he couldn't take it with him. The word *galled* means
   - ☐ a. annoyed.
   - ☐ b. entertained.
   - ☐ c. refused.

2. Although Uncle Basil never used the mail or the telephone, no one objected since people who are very rich are allowed their foibles. What are *foibles*?
   - ☐ a. friends or acquaintances
   - ☐ b. strengths or abilities
   - ☐ c. weak points or faults

3. There were instructions in his will for a funeral repast—beef, turkey, oysters, and lobsters. Define the word *repast*.
   - ☐ a. ceremony
   - ☐ b. meal
   - ☐ c. restaurant

4. When the lawyer opened the envelope, they saw one sentence in Uncle Basil's scrawl. The word *scrawl* means
   - ☐ a. careless handwriting.
   - ☐ b. vest pocket.
   - ☐ c. loose-leaf notebook.

☐ × 5 = ☐
NUMBER   YOUR
CORRECT   SCORE

☐ × 5 = ☐
NUMBER   YOUR
CORRECT   SCORE

IDENTIFYING STORY ELEMENTS. The following questions check your knowledge of story elements. Put an *x* in the box next to each correct answer.

1. Uncle Basil is best *characterized* as
   ☐ a. noble.
   ☐ b. affectionate.
   ☐ c. cheap.

2. Which of the following *foreshadows* the ending of the story?
   ☐ a. The members of the family flattered Uncle Basil to win his goodwill.
   ☐ b. Uncle Basil let Verner run errands for him.
   ☐ c. Again and again the family warned Uncle Basil, "You can't take it with you."

3. The *mood* of "You Can't Take It with You" is
   ☐ a. humorous.
   ☐ b. serious.
   ☐ c. terrifying.

4. Which sentence best expresses the *theme* of the story?
   ☐ a. It always pays to be pleasant to a wealthy relative.
   ☐ b. Despite what his family maintains, a miser manages to "take" his fortune with him.
   ☐ c. A miser leaves his housekeeper and his secretary generous gifts.

LOOKING AT CLOZE. The following questions use the cloze technique to check your reading comprehension. Complete the paragraph by filling in each blank with one of the words listed below. Each word appears in the story. Since there are five words and four blanks, one of the words will not be used.

In 1848 gold was _____ at Sutter's Mill in California, setting off a "gold rush" in the state. From everywhere, a _____ number of prospectors hurried to Sutter's Mill in the hope of establishing a claim. Although very few newcomers actually found gold, some local _____ people did become rich. They made their _____ by charging sky-high prices for food, lodging, and other necessities.

vast   gratitude

fortune

found   business

☐ × 5 = ☐
NUMBER CORRECT   YOUR SCORE

☐ × 5 = ☐
NUMBER CORRECT   YOUR SCORE

137

LEARNING HOW TO READ CRITICALLY.
The following questions check your critical
thinking skills. Put an *x* in the box next to
each correct answer.

1. Uncle Basil's actions suggest that he
   ☐ a. was very fond of his family.
   ☐ b. didn't care much for his family.
   ☐ c. was generous to all of his relatives
   and friends.

2. We may infer that the thick envelopes that
   lined Uncle Basil's coffin contained
   ☐ a. business papers.
   ☐ b. letters and remembrances from the
   people he loved.
   ☐ c. cash.

3. It is fair to say that Uncle Basil made sure
   that his coffin was roomy because he
   ☐ a. could afford the biggest and best
   coffin available.
   ☐ b. was an extremely large man.
   ☐ c. wanted to be certain there was
   enough room for his fortune.

4. At the conclusion of the story, the family
   probably felt
   ☐ a. satisfied.
   ☐ b. disappointed.
   ☐ c. relieved.

Improving Writing and Discussion Skills

- Describe how Uncle Basil managed
  to "take" his fortune with him. Explain
  why he told Verner to tack blue cloth
  on the sides and the bottom of the
  coffin.
- When Verner suggested that Uncle
  Basil's coffin be replaced with a better
  one, the family refused since the coffin
  "would only be burned." Suppose the
  family had bought a new coffin. How
  might the story have ended?
- Irony occurs when something happens that is the opposite of what might
  naturally be expected. What is ironic
  in "You Can't Take It with You"? Refer
  to Uncle Basil's last message to his
  family when you answer the question.

Use the boxes below to total your scores
for the exercises. Then write your score on
pages 140 and 141.

☐ SELECTING DETAILS FROM THE STORY
  +
☐ KNOWING NEW VOCABULARY WORDS
  +
☐ IDENTIFYING STORY ELEMENTS
  +
☐ LOOKING AT CLOZE
  +
☐ LEARNING HOW TO READ CRITICALLY
  ▼
☐ Score Total: Story 15

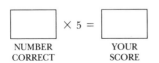

☐ × 5 = ☐

NUMBER   YOUR
CORRECT   SCORE

138

Acknowledgments

Acknowledgment is gratefully made to the following publishers, authors, and agents for permission to reprint these works. Adaptations and abridgments are by Burton Goodman.

"Three Skeleton Key" by George G. Toudouze. Reprinted by permission of *Esquire* magazine and the Hearst Corporation.

"The Marble Champ" by Gary Soto. From *Baseball in April and Other Stories,* © 1990 by Gary Soto, reprinted by permission of Harcourt Brace & Company.

"Phut Phat Concentrates" by Lilian Jackson Braun. Reprinted by The Putnam Berkley Group from *The Cat Who Had 14 Tales* by Lilian Jackson Braun. © 1988 by Lilian Jackson Braun.

"A Day's Wait" by Ernest Hemingway. Reprinted with permission of Charles Scribner's Sons, an imprint of Macmillan Publishing Company, from *Winner Takes Nothing* by Ernest Hemingway. © 1933 by Charles Scribner's Sons. Copyright renewed 1961 by Mary Hemingway.

"All the Years of Her Life" by Morley Callaghan. Reprinted by permission of the Estate of Morley Callaghan.

"The Love Letter" by Jack Finney. Reprinted by permission of Don Congdon Associates, Inc. © 1959, renewed 1987 by Jack Finney.

"Fly Like an Eagle" by Elizabeth Van Steenwyk. From *Fly Like an Eagle and Other Stories,* © 1978 by Elizabeth Van Steenwyk. Reprinted with permission from Walker and Company, 435 Hudson Street, New York, New York 10014, 1-800-289-2553. All rights reserved.

"Don't Tread on Me" by Walter Dean Myers. From *Mojo and the Russians* by Walter Dean Myers. Used by permission of Viking Penguin, a division of Penguin Books USA Inc.

"Say It with Flowers" by Toshio Mori. From *Yokohama California* by Toshio Mori. Reprinted by permission of The Caxton Printers, Ltd.

"The Story of the Widow's Son" by Mary Lavin. Copyright by Devin-Adair Publishers, Inc., Old Greenwich, Connecticut 06870. All rights reserved.

"Testimony of Trees" by Jesse Stuart. Copyright by Jesse Stuart and the Jesse Stuart Foundation. Adapted by permission of the Jesse Stuart Foundation, P.O. Box 391, Ashland, Kentucky 41114.

"You Can't Take It with You" by Eva-Lis Wuorio. From *Escape If You Can* by Eva-Lis Wuorio. © 1977 by Eva-Lis Wuorio. Used by permission of Viking Penguin, a division of Penguin Books USA Inc.

Progress Chart

1. Write in your score for each exercise.
2. Write in your Score Total.

	S	K	I	L	L	SCORE TOTAL
Story 1						
Story 2						
Story 3						
Story 4						
Story 5						
Story 6						
Story 7						
Story 8						
Story 9						
Story 10						
Story 11						
Story 12						
Story 13						
Story 14						
Story 15						

Progress Graph

1. Write your Score Total in the box under the number for each story.
2. Put an *x* along the line above each box to show your Score Total for that story.
3. Make a graph of your progress by drawing a line to connect the *x*'s.

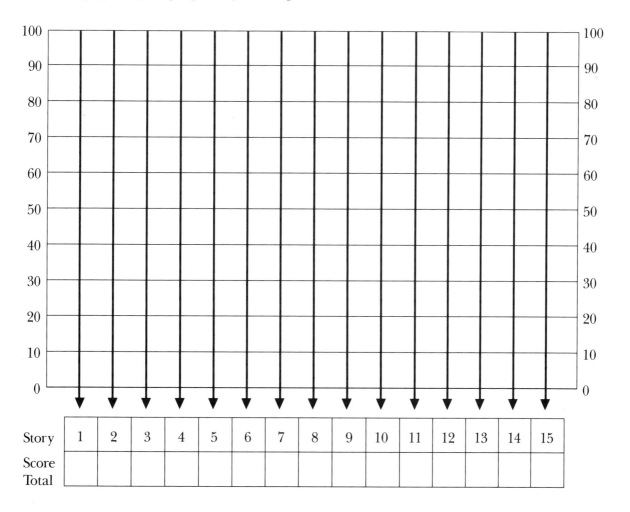

Story	1	2	3	4	5	6	7	8	9	10	11	12	13	14	15
Score Total															